MODERN PSYCHOLOGY

MODERN PSYCHOLOGY

The Teachings of Carl Gustav Jung

by
David Cox

Formerly published as TEACH YOURSELF ANALYTICAL PSYCHOLOGY

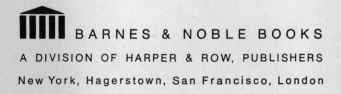

BARNES & NOBLE BOOKS

A DIVISION OF HARPER & ROW, PUBLISHERS

New York, Hagerstown, San Francisco, London

82 83 84 85 86   10 9 8

CONTENTS

v

FOREWORD

THERE is no doubt that there is immense value to be gained
from an understanding of Jung. But it is a formidable
task to begin a study of his psychology from his original
works. As a Jungian analyst I am often asked to recom-
mend books which make his ideas accessible at an introduc-
tory level. There are few such books, and I do not know of
any that gives a fair picture of the elements of Jungian
psychology with so much clarity and simplicity as this one
does. The author is not himself an analyst, and it is perhaps for this very reason that he is at so much pains to
clarify or dispense with technical terminology.

One of the most baffling problems for the layman is to
find his bearings among the many different views that appear
in the name of psychology. In order to meet this need,
the first three chapters of the book define the subject matter
of psychology, and outline contemporary theories other than
those of Jung. Chapter four describes aspects of psychic
functioning recognised by most therapeutic schools. Chapters five to nine elucidate the central concepts of Jungian
psychology. And the last chapter gives a brief account of
the author's impression of analysis.

All good teaching is an art, and bears within it something
original from the personality of the teacher. This book
is no exception. It has a certain bias. It is more concerned with the nature of man and his need for self-knowledge than with clinical conditions of sickness and health.
This approach is a valuable one, because Jung's researches
were immensely varied, and have a significance far beyond
the narrow confines of medical or curative psychology.

It might however be of interest if I were to indicate some
of the differences of emphasis that are part of my own bias
as an analyst. The analyst is in contact with the inner life
of individuals over long periods of time, and therefore sees
the unconscious mind as a living process which has both
continuity and purposiveness. The symbols and symbol-

making activity of the unconscious mind are ever-present realities. Conscious mind, on the other hand, has far less power, effectiveness and continuity. It dies every night in sleep, and is modified by conditions of health, fatigue and a variety of other influences from within and without. To the analyst it often seems that the fluctuations of consciousness, rather than of the unconscious, might be described as "odd things".

Nevertheless, the mind as a whole has what Jung calls "psychic reality", which is different from the material reality of the body and the external world, but which is known to exist both because we "experience" it and because of its effects in the external world.

For practical analysis, dreams are an important part of the reality of the mind. When a dream is rightly interpreted, the conscious mind is enlarged and strengthened by new insights. It is possible that the understanding of a single dream may bring about a transformation of the personality. A series of dreams may be shown to have a continuity of meaning, which is not only helpful to the patient but which also suggests that "meaning" is an inherent characteristic of the human mind. The realisation of "meaning" requires the co-operation of both the conscious and the unconscious mind.

Jung found that a "sense of meaning in life" was essential to human health, happiness and even sanity. At different stages of the life cycle the content of this meaning changes. In the first half of life, meaning is concerned with the establishment of the ego, the fulfilment of biological needs and duties, and the achievement of a place in the world. In the second half of life the sphere of meaning shifts to the goal of inner understanding. Not everyone arrives at this stage of understanding. Those who do, experience a process of development which Jung called Individuation. As a result of Individuation the personality is reintegrated as a unique whole, in which the ego is subordinated to something greater than itself within the psyche. This greater something Jung called the Self.

It will be apparent that the points I have mentioned are all concerned with the mind as it unfolds in the dimension of time and in the life-cycle of the individual.   This is the bias of the analyst, who is always confronted with the psychology of a particular individual at a particular time of life in a particular life-situation.   The task of the analyst is to help his patient to find the meaning of his life, which has been lost because consciousness and the unconscious are no longer co-operating.

None of these points is neglected by the author.   But in his exposition he has subordinated the time dimension to the structural aspects of the psyche.   This has been a wise and careful selection, because it has enabled him to present with a remarkable simplicity and clarity a subject which is in fact immensely complex.   Anyone who is familiar with the vast range and profundity of Jung's thought will appreciate the nature of the author's achievement.

Faye Pye
B.A. Cantab., M.A.(Psych.), Lond.,
L.R.C.P., M.R.C.S.

Chapter I: WHAT IS PSYCHOLOGY?

Thought

PSYCHOLOGY is primarily concerned with what goes on in the mind. For example, when someone is afraid, all sorts of this are happening at once and some of them are the concern of psychology. When a man is afraid electrical currents are passing between the cells of his brain, and along his nervous system; a chemical substance called adrenalin is being pumped into his bloodstream; he is "feeling afraid". When we think about what it means to "be afraid" we may think about any of these things, and they are all somehow connected together. If adrenalin is artificially introduced into someone's bloodstream it is found that he feels afraid, even though there is nothing for him to be afraid of. Whether what we are doing when we think about being afraid and things like that is "psychology" or not depends upon what we are thinking about, and upon the way in which we think about it.

It is quite possible for someone to think about fear without thinking about the feeling of "being afraid" at all. He might simply examine the electrical discharges in the brain and the nervous system, and see how they are related to each other and to the bodily movements of the man who is afraid. A person who thought about fear in this way would not be thinking about it psychologically, because this way of thinking about what happens is called "neurology" which means the study of the nervous system.   Someone else might choose to study the way in which the glands of the body produce adrenalin when we are afraid, and this would be "bio-chemistry", that is, the study of the chemistry of living things.   We should only speak of "psychology" when what is being thought about is the actual feeling "inside" of "being afraid"—although when one is thinking psychologically one may try to see how this feeling is connected with the brain, the nervous system and the glands.   Psychology is concerned with what goes on in our minds, and we should always remember that this is different from what happens in our brains. The things with which psychology is concerned are things like fear, thinking, hoping, making decisions and so on.

Behaviour

Psychology is also concerned with many of the things which people do.   If an unarmed man meets a lion he is likely to be afraid, and when someone is afraid he is likely to turn and run.   When someone who is afraid runs away from the thing he is frightened of it is obvious that there is some connection between that person's fear and his running away.   Just as we can think of being afraid in several different ways, so we can think of its connection with running away in different ways.   For example, one can discover how the adrenalin which is produced influences a man's ability to run, or one can wonder what sort of images occur in the man's mind as he runs: the first way of thinking about it belongs to bio-chemistry, the second to psychology. If one thinks that the running away is somehow caused by the man's fear, or that it is in some way an expression of that fear, then the running away is part of psychology, because the man's behaviour is thought of as the result of what is happening in his mind. In other words psychology is often about what people do as well as about what they think or "feel".

Although psychology is often concerned with human behaviour it is not concerned with all kinds of behaviour. For instance, when a doctor is examining a patient he may tap the leg just below the knee, and if the patient is normal his foot will kick forward. This is known as a "reflex" and so far as we know it is a purely physical response on the part of the nervous system in the region of the knee. It does not appear to be connected either with the brain or the mind. Reflexes of this kind that are part of the mechanics of the human body are not usually the concern of psychologists—although sometimes there may be psychological reasons which prevent such reflexes from occurring.

If someone trips at the top of the stairs and falls down them one can examine the ways in which his body fell and the "mechanics" of his tumble, and this would not be psychology at all. If the head of the staircase was dark and there was some unexpected slippery thing at the top, then it is difficult to see how any study of the fall could be psychological. On the other hand, if the fall occurred in the person's own house, on a well-lit staircase that he had often used one might well look for psychological reasons for his fall on that particular occasion. These illustrations show how the study of behaviour is often psychology, and also how difficult it may be to see when behaviour should be studied in this way and when it should not. The general rule is that the study of behaviour is psychological when what a person does is done because he is the particular person he is, and not merely because his body is influenced by some kind of force from outside.

Perception

When we speak of "behaviour" we are inclined to think of things which we call "actions", things which we "do" *and know* that we do. There is another kind of behaviour which goes on most of the time which we do not often notice. Sitting down, standing up or walking along we are always taking some sort of note of our surroundings. We notice the chairs and tables in a room, the shops as we walk along the street and the people whom we meet. We do not only do things to the world around us, we also take note of what that world is like. This kind of behaviour is called "perceiving" or "perception" and like being afraid it is something which we can think of psychologically and also in other ways.

A man goes into his garden in daylight and he sees a red rose. At first we think that this is something very simple, because most of our waking life we are seeing something or other, but when we begin to think about what seems to happen we realise that it is not at all simple. The man would not be able to see a rose or anything else unless light was shining upon it, and we are told that some of the light which shines on the rose is reflected from the rose into his eyes. The light rays falling upon his eyes are focused by the lenses in them and concentrated on the retina at their back: the optic nerve is stimulated by the concentrated light rays, and an electrical discharge along the nerve produces electrical movements in his brain, and the frequency of those movements is connected with the colour of the rose which he sees. At the same time he is aware of what we call "seeing" the rose, and what he sees is not just a patch of colour, but something which he recognises as "a rose". When we speak of "perception" we are speaking of the whole business of becoming aware of a rose—or anything else—and it includes the fact that we distinguish the things which we see, as well as that we are aware of seeing different patches of colour.

It is obvious that physics and neurology are both sciences which enable us to think about perception, and that there are many things about perception which are not the proper things for psychology to study. At the same time the fact that we are aware that we are seeing a rose, for example, is clearly a fact about what is going on in our minds, and so it is something which we must take note of when we are thinking psychologically.

Hallucination

When we think about perception we should also think about hallucination. We say that we perceive something when there is something "there" and we see it, but sometimes it seems to people that they see something (or hear or touch it) when there is nothing "there" to be seen, and this is called "hallucination". If we are certain that there is no reasonable physical explanation of an hallucination it is something which we can think about psychologically, because we can ask why that particular person should have come to think he saw the thing he did.

There are some occasions when we seem to become aware of something which is not there which is not the concern of psychology at all. The easiest illustration is that of someone who has had a leg cut off. A person who has lost his leg still feels pains and cramps and movements in the toes of the foot which is not there, and this appears to be simply explained by thinking about the nervous system. The nerves which carry "messages" between the foot and the brain pass all the way through the body, and when the leg is cut off they are only cut, they are not wholly removed. Suppose, for example, the telephone line between London and Edinburgh is cut at Rugby, and a message is sent along it from Rugby to London. If the person who received the message at London does not know that the line has been cut he has no way of telling the difference between the message from Rugby and one that has come from Edinburgh, all he knows is that the message has come along the line from Edinburgh. In the same way the nerves from foot to brain may be cut off at the knee, but they still exist between knee and brain, and stimulation of those nerves at the place where they have been cut will produce the impression of pains and movements in the (no longer existing) foot.

Forms of Psychology

All psychology is concerned with our thoughts, with much of our active behaviour and with our perceptions of the outside world, but there are a very large number of different ways of studying these things. "Psychology" is not one science, but a name which includes a great number of different sciences all of which are concerned with the same sort of things. "Psychology" may mean thinking about the nature of our mental activities like hoping, wanting and making decisions; it may mean studying the words which we use to talk about these things; it may mean a survey of the way in which people actually think or behave; and it may mean the consideration of the way in which people can be helped when something has gone wrong with their minds. In this book we shall be concerned with one special form of psychology, but in this chapter we shall give a brief indication of one or two of the other forms which psychology takes.

Philosophical Psychology

Certain people once said that the only thing which anyone ever wants is "pleasure", and that all desires are desires for pleasure. We are not concerned whether this is true or not, it is simply an illustration of the kind of thinking which can be called "Philosophical Psychology". Psychology of this sort is the attempt to understand more clearly the things which go. on all the time, which we know about very well, but which turn out to be quite complicated when we really start to think about them. Such things include, for example, the business of making a choice or decision. How is it that when we have to decide between several different things to do we choose to do one and not the other? How far does our "sense of duty", our "conscience" or our moral standard influence us? and how do we manage to decide between doing something that we want to do very much and something that we do not want to do, but believe we ought to do? If we say that we are "free to choose" between alternatives do we merely mean that circumstances do not force a choice upon us, or do we mean something more than this? If we do what we do because we are the sort of person that we are, can we also be said to have been "free" to do something different? Philosophers have been asking questions like this for a very, very long time, usually in connection with problems of behaviour, and any study of this kind is psychology.

Philosophy in England today pays a great deal of attention to the way in which we use words, and this has its effect on philosophical psychology. Psychology of this sort may be concerned with what we mean by words like "fear" and "hate". We often talk as though "hate" were something that a man has inside him, but it is difficult to see just what this means. It can be suggested that when we talk about "hate" we are simply talking about people's thoughts and behaviour. If John hates Jack, it may be said: That means that John speaks in a nasty way when he is talking to Jack, thinks with pleasure of unpleasant things happening to Jack, will not go out of his way to help Jack, may even hinder him and so on;—and this is all that we mean by "hate". Once again it does not matter whether this is a true account of what we mean by a word like "hate", it is merely an example of the sort of thing with which philosophical psychologists may be concerned.

Statistical Psychology

Not very long ago Kinsey produced two large books about people's sexual behaviour. In his introduction he pointed out that before we talk too much about how people ought to behave in connection with sex it would be a good thing to try to find out how they do behave. In order to do this he collected evidence from a very large number of people and arranged the results "statistically": for example, he gave the proportion of married men in his sample between the ages of (say) thirty and forty who had sexual relations with women other than their wives. Much statistical psychology is done by means of widespread enquiries intended to find out how people behave or think in connection with one thing or another. The results of such enquiries are arranged in such a way that they show patterns of behaviour—all those who behave in a similar way are grouped together, and this grouping is then compared with other ways of grouping the same people, such as social background, living in town or country, having brothers or sisters, being only children, and so on.

The multitudinous tests used for so many purposes nowadays are also part of statistical psychology. Intelligence tests are designed to compare the ability of people to distinguish and relate the material with which they are presented; there are personality tests designed to show degrees of neurosis, or the extent of introversion or extraversion; tests are carried out to compare perceptive ability in normal circumstances with the same ability in special circumstances—for instance in emergency or under drugs. The field of statistical psychology is as large as the field of human behaviour, and a great amount of work is being done in connection with it. The thing which distinguishes this kind of psychology from most other kinds is that it is concerned with the general or "normal" behaviour of a large number of people, and not with the peculiarities of the individual. In this respect statistical psychology is the opposite of psychotherapy which is concerned with the problems of the individual, and of which we shall have much to say in later chapters.

Behaviourist Psychology

We decide what sort of person someone else is by seeing how that person behaves, and our own behaviour is a very clear indication of what we are. People's behaviour is a good guide to their inner nature, and a study of someone's behaviour may tell us a great deal about what that person is. It may also be said that for most purposes and from most points of view what a person does is more important than what is going on in his mind, and that the real importance of what goes on in the mind is the way in which it affects behaviour. Because of this when behaviour is thought of as an expression of a man's inner nature there is reason for regarding the study of behaviour as a form of psychology. "Behaviourism" however has become the name of a special attitude to psychology, and it is usually connected with a particular opinion which is called "Epiphenomenalism".

Everyone must admit that there is some connection between the way a person behaves and what is going on in his mind. If someone sees that the edge of the cliff on which he is standing is about to crumble he will jump away from it, and at the same time he will have a feeling of fright, or an awareness of danger. Some people would say that he sees what is about to happen, realises the danger, feels afraid and, *as a result*, moves quickly away. In other words some people would say that his (mental) awareness of danger is the cause of his running away. Those who hold the theory called "epiphenomenalism" deny this: they say that there is a direct connection between the sight of the falling cliff and the jumping away and that this connection has nothing to do with the sense of danger or the feeling of fear. Such people say that the feeling of fear is something which happens at the same time as the sight of danger and the jumping away, but that it does not cause the person to run away. According to them jumping away is a reflex action which occurs when the cliff is seen to be about to fall.

The ideas behind this view can best be illustrated by

the well-known experiments which Pavlov and others did with dogs.   The kind of thing done was to put a dog in a cage at one end of a wired-in run and a plate of food at the other end.   When the cage was opened, the dog ran to the food and ate.   Then the experiment was repeated, and when the food was put in position a circular disc was displayed: at other times an empty plate was put down and a square shown. After this had been done many times it was found that the dog would run out of its cage when a circular disc was shown and stay in its cage when a square was shown, whether or not food was put down at the same time.   The natural reaction of the dog to food had been transferred, by a process of conditioning, to the differently shaped tokens, and the reflex response to the tokens was known as a "conditioned reflex".   The idea of a "conditioned reflex" is used by behaviourists to explain the great majority of human actions.

Most of us do not think that the ideas of behaviourists are satisfactory, but although we may not be ready to think that all human behaviour can be explained in terms of reflex action to the situations in which we find ourselves, it is as well to realise that a great deal of behaviour can be explained in this way.   Children who have become accustomed to the way their school is run do not need to stop and think when the bell is rung after break; they simply move towards their class-rooms, and this is a reflex action to the bell.   We do not think about cleaning our teeth every night, but at a certain stage of the business of going to bed we reach for our toothbrush.

The attitude of behaviourists can be illustrated in

practice by the example of a psychologist who devised a cure for writer's cramp. Writer's cramp is the inability to hold pen or pencil in order to write with it, and the assumption was made that this was the result of some unpleasant experience associated with writing. The object of the cure was to "uncondition" the reflex by associating something equally unpleasant with failing to write. In order to do this a simple apparatus was designed: the patient attempted to trace out lines or letters with a steel instrument held like a pen, and when he failed to trace them correctly he received a sharp electric shock. It was claimed that this apparatus did in fact produce satisfactory results and made people suffering from writer's cramp able to write freely again.

Therapeutic Psychology

All the forms of psychology of which we have spoken are concerned with examining or thinking about the way in which people think or behave. It may be that as a result of such examination suggestions can be made which may help people to overcome difficulties of thought or behaviour (as we saw in the case of the attempted cure of writer's cramp, based on the theories of behaviourist psychology), but if this does happen it is more or less accidental. The aim of all these forms of psychology is more accurate knowledge about the way our minds work and the way in which we behave. The kind of psychology with which we shall be concerned in the rest of this book is concerned with the actual problems of individuals who need help, and it is called "Psychotherapy", because "therapy" means "healing".   This kind of psychology starts in the consulting room, when an individual patient is seeking healing because of some trouble which has upset his normal living.   Such a patient does not want to be told any theories or ideas about psychology, what he wants is real practical help.

Most kinds of psychotherapy have two aspects. On the one hand there is the way in which the psychotherapist tries to help the patient, that is, what actually goes on in the consulting room.   This is the first and most important thing, and everything else in psychotherapy is somehow connected with it.   At the same time if psychotherapists are to learn more about their work and to benefit from each other's experience, they have to understand what they are doing as well as do it.   This means that psychotherapy includes the development of ideas about what is going on during psychological treatment, about the way in which the mind should work, and about the way in which it does work.   In other words psychotherapy includes a great deal of theory, and we shall have something to say about this in later chapters.

It is sometimes suggested that psychological theories which have grown out of the attempt to cure people suffering from mental diseases are of little importance to people who are "normal", but it is easy to see why this view is wrong.   The doctor who seeks to heal diseased bodies would be able to do very little if he had no idea how the body ought to work when it was not diseased (for one reason, he would not even be able to tell if his patients were suffering from a disease or not), and much the same is true of psychotherapists. But it is also true that it is by no means clear that anyone *is* "normal", if "normal" means "without any kind of disturbance of the most efficient working of the mind possible". On the whole it seems most likely that those who are in urgent need of psychological help are suffering from an exaggerated form of a difficulty which occurs again and again in a less violent way in people who are perfectly "normal"— in the sense of not being noticeably different from a great many other people.

Psychiatry

All psychotherapy has developed from medicine, but there are two main forms, "psychiatry" and "psychological analysis". It is not always easy to draw a line between the two, and it should be said that most psychiatrists make some use of the methods of analysis, and that some analysts do occasionally resort to the methods of psychiatry. Psychiatry is more directly connected with the work of medical doctors, and is carried out on similar lines.

Although psychiatry is concerned with disorders of the mind it is very closely connected with neurology, and the psychiatrist often attempts to influence the mind by working on the brain. The two most obvious instances of this are "electrical shock therapy" and "leucotomy". Shock therapy is designed to give a violent disturbance to the brain in such a way that the things which prevent its proper functioning are cleared away; leucotomy is an operation by which various parts of the brain which appear to be causing serious disorder are cut off from the rest, so that they no longer interfere with it—very much as a doctor may feel that it is necessary to amputate an infected limb to prevent it from poisoning the rest of the body. Psychiatrists may also employ drugs, long periods of sleep and other physical means in order to attempt to help their patients.   And, as we have said, there are psychiatrists who rely largely on the methods used by psychological analysts.

Psychological Analysis

One way in which psychological analysis differs from most psychiatric practice is that no use is made of physical means.   The idea is to deal directly with the mind of the patient, and the treatment could be described as a "talking cure", because the only really satisfactory way of getting to know the mind of someone else is by talking to that person.   It should be added, however, that there are some analysts who are ready to make use of the methods of psychiatry when they think that they may aid the "talking cure".   For example, an analyst might believe that when it seemed impossible to talk to a particular patient at all some form of shock theraphy might make this possible, and some analysts believe that the talking can be carried out more effectively when the patient is under some drug such as lycurgic acid.   In general, however, the analyst does his work through talks with the patient.

In the end psychological analysis is concerned with only one thing, and that is the patient's knowledge of himself, and in this it is a long way removed from traditional medicine. On the whole what is important in medicine as it has been practiced in the past, is that the doctor should correctly diagnose the disease from which the patient is suffering, and know how to cure it: he may well give the patient a great deal of information about the disease and about the methods of cure, but one does not usually imagine that the success of the cure depends upon whether the patient understands what is going on or not. Penicillin will destroy harmful germs within the human body whether the patient knows anything or nothing about what is causing his trouble, or about the action of penicillin. Analysis is pointless unless the patient discovers things about his own mind which he did not know before, and this is why psychological analysis always takes a very long time.

The job of an analyst is to help the patient to discover things about himself for himself, and like all learning processes the speed at which this happens depends upon the patient. It is no good for the analyst to keep telling the patient things which the patient is not able to understand or ready to accept: he (the analyst) must patiently wait and watch while the patient gradually comes to understand more and more. At the same time the analyst should have knowledge gained from study and experience which enables him to say the right thing at the right time— although no analyst would claim to be infallible.

Chapter II: PSYCHOANALYSIS AND ANALYTICAL PSYCHOLOGY

Analysts

AT the present time no one has to have any qualifications before he can offer to help people by means of psychological analysis. Doctors have a medical degree and psychiatrists are doctors who have had psychiatric training and experience, and have achieved quite definite psychiatric qualifications. An analyst may have medical or psychiatric qualifications but he does not have to have any. Analysts who are not also medical doctors are frequently referred to as "lay analysts".

It is obviously not altogether satisfactory for anyone to be able to claim to be a psychological analyst, and attempts are made to prevent it. Analysts form societies and set out strict rules which must be complied with before anyone can become a member of the society—but it must be repeated that it is not necessary to be a member of such a society in order to do the work of an analyst. Two such societies are the Institute of Psychoanalysis and the Society of Analytical Psychologists: the members of the first claim to be following the ideas of Sigmund Freud, those of the second claim to be following the ideas of Carl Gustav Jung. On the whole the tendency is to encourage would-be members to get a degree in medicine before becoming analysts, but for various reasons the rules normally allow lay analysts to become members as well.

There is one unbreakable rule which both societies insist upon, and that is that the would-be analyst should himself have a full psychological analysis. This is an obviously important rule, and it is not only one which must be kept by anyone who wants to be a member of a society of analysts, it is also a necessity for anyone who wants to be accepted as a responsible analyst by other analysts, whether he is a member of a society or not.

Freud and Jung

Modern psychological analysis was invented at the turn of the century, and its early home was in Vienna. It was developed out of the attempts to cure hysteria and other nervous diseases by hypnotism and similar methods which were practised by doctors in Paris. The first work was done by Sigmund Freud, and it can be claimed that the basic principles of modern psychotherapy were discovered by him. They were made widely known by such books of his as *The Interpretation of Dreams* and *The Psychopathology of Everyday Life*.

A Swiss doctor, Carl Gustav Jung, was working on very similar lines in the treatment of nervous diseases, and he was very impressed by Freud's work. So much so that the two men became colleagues. After a while they found that they could not agree about things which were basic to the work they were doing, and they were forced to separate: the result of that separa-

tion is that there are now two great schools of psychotherapy, one developing the ideas of Freud, and the
other those of Jung.

One cannot help feeling that the emotional tension
which accompanied the breach between Freud and
Jung has resulted in a wider cleavage between the
schools of psychology derived from the work of the
two men than need have been the case, but on the
other hand one should not overestimate the gulf
between these two schools.   There are a very large
number of analysts who would not say that they were
either "Freudian" or "Jungian", but would claim that
they had learnt from the ideas of both men, and also
from many others.   Moreover many who do claim
to be "Freudian" analysts have incorporated many of
Jung's ideas into their thought, and there are plenty
of "Jungians" who openly acknowledge their debt to
Freud and his disciples, in particular to Melanie
Klein.   Nevertheless, despite the readiness on the part
of analysts to learn from both schools and from other
analysts, it remains true that there are very marked
differences between the two schools, and these differences are clearly shown by the difference in the terms
used.

Terms

Suppose two people are looking at a flower garden.
The first one is impressed by the formal lay-out of the
flower-beds and the grass between the beds and the
paths which wind about.   He talks about the massed

flowers and the dividing paths in terms of the shape of the beds, and of their relationship to each other.   The other one is interested in the care with which the gardener has arranged the different colours of the flowers, and the way that they contrast with the green grass and the brown paths.   The two people talk about the garden in quite a different way, and use different terms to talk about it: the first one uses terms which refer to shape and size, the second uses terms which refer to depth of colour and contrasts of colour.   They are both talking about the same garden and they both say true things about the garden, but they say very different things about it.   If they go further, and each one insists that his way of looking at and talking about the garden is the most satisfactory way of doing these things, then there may be a real conflict between them even thought they both admit that what the other person says is also true (but not so helpful).   This is something like the situation in psychotherapy.   The Freudians and the Jungians both give different accounts of the structure of the human mind, and their accounts are different because they see different ways of arranging the things which go on in the human mind.   The terms they use are different because they bring out the different ways of arranging these things, and each group is inclined to claim that their own terms, that is, their own way of thinking about the mind, is the better way.   The difference in terms does result from a real difference of opinion.

The difference between the picture of the human mind given by the two large schools of psychology is so great that a Freudian analyst has been reported as saying that he could not recognise any of the features in the Jungian account of the psyche, and this makes discussion between people of different schools very difficult.   In this book an attempt will be made to explain the terms used by Jungians, but it is as well to know something about those which are used by Freudians, and in this chapter a few of the main Freudian terms will be mentioned, and their meaning briefly indicated.   The following table is given as a very rough guide: the terms on the left have special meanings in Freudian psychology, those on the right have special meanings in Jungian psychology.

Freudian	Jungian
Psychoanalysis	Analytical Psychology
The superego	The personal unconscious
The Id	The collective unconscious
The subconscious	Archetypes
Libido	Psychic energy
	The Self

The lists could be greatly extended, but they should be long enough to give most people some clue to the attitude of those who write and talk about psychology: if the terms on the left are frequently used the ideas are likely to be Freudian, if the terms on the right keep coming up the ideas are likely to be Jungian.   There are of course many other terms which are used by all psychotherapists of whatever school—terms like "repression", "the transference", "the psyche" and "the unconscious".

It should be noticed that in the above table there are

only two pairs of terms which correspond: "psycho-analysis" and "analytical psychology" are both names for a school of psychology, and "libido" and "psychic energy" have very similar meanings: on the other hand "superego", "id" and "subconscious" provide a way of breaking up the psyche into "blocks" which is quite different from the way in which it is divided when Jung's terms are used. We shall try to explain the terms common to psychotherapists of all schools, and those special to Jungians in later chapters, in this chapter we shall give a very brief explanation of the terms in the left-hand column above.

Psychoanalysis

"Psychoanalysis" is popularly used to mean any kind of analytical treatment, and it is obvious that it would be a very satisfactory word for this, if it had not become a technical term. For various historical reasons it has become the technical term to describe analytical work as it is done by those who regard themselves as in some sense disciples of Freud, and it should be kept strictly for use in this way. If we wish to talk about analytical work in general we may have to say "psychological analysis", or "depth analysis". The corresponding name for work carried out by those who are in some sense disciples of Jung is "Analytical Psychology". The existence of these two names is an indication of the fact that there are considerable basic differences between the two approaches to psychotherapy.

Superego

The story is told of a man who was drifting down the river at Cambridge and passed by a punt tied to the bank.   A man and a girl were talking, and the girl was heard to say "I don't see *how* I can go out with you if you really do not believe there is such a thing as a categorical imperative"!   We all know that there are certain principles which we feel must be respected, and that there are strong rules which we impose upon ourselves.   These rules are sometimes moral rules, but they are not always moral in the sense of being rules about good and evil.   For some people conventional rules have a stronger force than moral rules, and a man who regularly cheats at his business might be quite unable to sit down to his dinner unless he was wearing a collar and tie.   Sometimes the rules which we cannot break appear to be entirely arbitrary, and to have no good foundation at all.   A boy was once told that "you must never hit a screw with a hammer", and it was many years before he could bring himself to do this, even though it might be the most effective way of starting the screw off.

Apart from the rules and principles which we impose upon ourselves most people also have a picture of the person he is, or ought to be, in their minds, and judge their behaviour by the extent to which it conforms to that picture.   The rules and principles, and the ideal picture of what we ought to be can be thought of as a "person" inside us who has strong views about how we ought to behave, is always ready to criticise us when we do not behave in the right way, and does his best to make us do the right thing or punish us when we have done the wrong thing. Freudians refer to this "person" inside us as the "superego".

There is no doubt that the things connected with the idea of the superego happen, and it is often useful to have a term which enables us to lump them together. In other words there is no doubt that the term "superego" does refer to something that goes on in peoples' lives, but the use of the term means more than this. First of all, by calling all these things "parts of the superego" one suggests that they form a close-knit group and tend to reinforce one another, and at the same time one also suggest that they are all the same kind of thing. It is by no means certain that this is true. We may feel the force of convention as strongly as we feel the force of a moral principle, and we may be guided by arbitrary ideas of what "must" be done in much the same way as we are by convention and morals, but it does not necessarily follow that they are all the same sort of thing. The differences between them may be just as important as the likeness. According to Freudian ideas, they are not only alike, they also originate in the same way, and this is the second thing that is meant by using the term "superego".

The idea is that as we grow up we take into ourselves ideas and attitudes which are held by people around us. It cannot always be said exactly why we accept one idea and not another, although some of the reasons are clear enough. If a child loves his mother very much it is quite likely that he will accept, without question, her hopes about the sort of person she wants him to be, so that he takes over from her an ideal picture of himself; if some moral principle is told to a child with great emotional force it is likely to make a lasting impression on him; if certain conventions are accepted by everybody around him without question, a man grows up assuming that they must be followed at all times. In such ways as these, it is suggested, a part of the mind is formed which is the reflection inside us of all the people and groups which have contributed to it as we grew up—and this is what Freudians mean by the "super-ego".

The Id

"The Id" is the term which Freud uses for the raw material of our mental life, and which refers to the underlying, instinctive, animal part of our nature. The "id" contains the driving forces of our life, the desire for food and for sexual satisfaction, aggressive tendencies, tendencies to escape danger by flight or some other means and so on. The "id" is said to have no aim but the search for pleasure, and pleasure is said to mean the release of tension—as when we are hungry we feel a sense of strain and tension until we relieve our hunger by eating. The "id" has no thoughts of right and wrong and no ability to think about things—it can only distinguish between objects which it seeks, on the one hand, and those from which it tries to get away on the other. When the "id" cannot satisfy its desires it forms imaginative pictures of the things which would satisfy them.

All life-force comes from the "id", but in the course

of human development the failure to satisfy all the desires of the "id" leads to the formation of the "ego": this is the conscious mental being which we know ourselves to be, and the "ego" is capable of distinguishing objects in many different ways, of thinking, feeling, making plans and generally running a life. Whereas the "id" seeks to satisfy desires directly the "ego" is prepared to search for ways and means to do so: whereas the desires of the "id" are straightforward the "ego" is able to substitute one desire for another. Both the "id" and the "ego" are liable to be frustrated by the "superego", as well as to conflict with each other.

Once again no one can deny that there are in human beings those tendencies which Freud attributes to the "id", but to use the term "id" in this way is to claim that the stuff of our life is of a particular and limited kind—that at the root of human living there is nothing more than the search for the satisfaction of elementary needs which we share with animals, and that all else is due to the modification of those needs or to checks and controls which we have been forced to make as a result of our encounter with the world around. The Jungian view is sharply distinguished from these ideas in that Jung claims that the basic "stuff" of mental life (that which gives us power and direction) is not merely instinctive and pleasure-seeking but includes strivings towards the "heights", and is as much related to the most spiritual tendencies in men as it is to the most animal. In fact, some of those things which Freud regards as a part of the "superego" Jung thinks of as originating in the depths of human nature.

The Subconscious

In ordinary speech it is quite possible to use "subconscious" as an adjective: we can speak of subconscious thoughts, impressions, ideas and so on. When "the subconscious" is used as a noun it is a technical term which has a place in psychoanalysis, but not in analytical psychology. The Freudian idea of the subconscious can best be described as a dustbin into which we throw all the things in our mind which we do not want—though we must remember that things which have been thrown into the subconscious still have an effect on our lives. They may be out of sight, but they can influence our minds.

The subconscious includes the things one does not want, and also the things that one thinks one does not want. This means that there are two very good reasons for trying to do something about the subconscious. The first is that it is not a very satisfactory dust-bin because the things put into it have not been got rid of, but are liable to fester and cause a "nasty smell". The second is that it is quite possible that we may have made a mistake and that things which have been thrown away are really things which would be very valuable to us if we had kept them. The main reason why "the subconscious" is not a term used in Jungian psychology is that Jung is concerned to point out that the things which we manage to "lose" are not neatly shut off in a compartment of their own, but get mixed up with other things which we do not know about, and probably never have known about.   What this means will be explained later.

Libido

"Libido" means "desire," with a special reference to sexual desire and Freud originally used it with much this meaning for the drive and power behind human living.   In the early days of psychoanalysis he spoke as though our basic drive was entirely sexual, and that all other aims and desires arose by some modification of this sexual drive.   In the development of psychoanalysis this idea has changed considerably, and the term "libido" has lost a great deal of its original sexual meaning.   Freud himself pointed out that the sexual aspect of the basic drive *developed* in a person's early years, and this opened the way for "libido" to be thought of as energy which gradually takes on differentiated forms, and becomes directed to specific ends. The term "libido" is also freely used by Jung and Jungians, but it is used with even less sexual implication.   According to Jung the basic energy of a man (i.e. his "libido") is bound up with particular aims (of which sex is one, but only one) from the beginning.

The term "psychic energy" is often used with the same meaning as "libido", but when Jung introduced it he was attempting to form the idea of a quantity of energy or power which could be measured and compared, even though it appeared in different forms. In trying to do this he was copying the idea of "energy" used in physics.   In physics, for example, we say that a moving body has a certain amount of energy simply because it is moving, and we also say that an electric battery has a certain amount of energy because we know that we can use the battery to light a lamp or run an electric motor, and we can compare the energy of the battery with that of a moving body, even though the *kind* of energy is quite different.   Psychic energy is not possessed by moving bodies and electric batteries but by emotions, ideas in the the mind, instincts and so on, and in using the term "energy" Jung hoped that it might be possible to measure the amount of energy that such things have, and to compare the psychic energy of, say, a strong desire with that of an ingrained habit.   This means that psychic energy ought to be thought of as quantity without quality (i.e. as a measure of how much, not an indication of the kind of thing possessing energy), but psychic energy always appears in the form of some particular psychic drive, and this is why the term "psychic energy" can be used in much the same way as "libido".

It should be said again that this brief account of a few Freudian terms is only an outline intended to give some idea of how they are used, and to distinguish them from the terms of Analytical Psychology.   It is not only the terms and the ideas which are different, the actual methods and techniques of the two schools are different as well.

Technique

Many people probably have a vague picture of psychological analysis in action.   The "traditional" picture is that of the analyst's couch, on which the patient lies in a room with the lights dimmed while the analyst keeps as far out of the patient's sight as possible.   This picture is not true of Jungian analysis but it is largely true of psychoanalysis.   Psycho-analysts keep very close to the idea of doctor and patient: in the analysis the problems and difficulties are the problems and difficulties of the patient, the mind which is being dealt with is the mind of the patient and the analyst remains "outside" that mind and its problems, probing here, diagnosing there and offering sugges-tions when needed.   The detachment of the analyst is a basic principle of Freudian psychology.

Jung's principles are rather different from this, and Jungian analysis is based upon the idea that the analyt-ical situation is a personal encounter in which two minds act upon each other.   In other words the Jungian psychologist starts with the assumption that he cannot remain detached from what is happening to the patient, and that his own personality influences the patient to a considerable extent.   Whereas the Freudian analyst attempts to bring his knowledge and skill to the work, the Jungian analyst is aware that as well as doing this he is entering into a personal en-counter with his patient, and that he is not only using his knowledge and skill but also throwing his person-ality into the work.   There is no doubt that this exposes the analyst to many and great dangers, but most analysts (at any rate, most Jungian analysts) would admit that their work is a matter of walking along a knife-edge, and they would say that the risk of danger was the cost which has to be paid for doing or trying to do anything worth while.

Chapter III: CONSCIOUSNESS, THE UNCONSCIOUS AND THE PSYCHE

What we know ourselves to be

Before attempting to think about the unconscious it is as well to have some idea of what we mean by "consciousness", or "the conscious mind". We all know what consciousness is, because it is ourselves as we know ourselves when we think of ourselves as mental beings, but it is not at all easy to describe the things which make up consciousness. Any account of consciousness is likely to be a very personal matter and to suffer from the peculiarities of the person formulating it, but this is not of very great importance because other people can correct the errors and omissions by thinking about their own minds. One way of indicating the nature of consciousness is to describe it under five heads—

1. *Life aims*

A boy may be determined to become the pilot of an aeroplane; a politician may hope and be determined to become prime minister; a young man may intend to "do the best for himself" and get a job paying good money; a man may intend to make his mark in the world and get fame; another man may aim to be a good respectable citizen, with a wife and family, a pleasant house and an attractive garden; older people may seek no more than to hold down the job they are in, to do effectively the work that lies before them, or to "get the most out of life". The great majority of people have one or more overriding aims for their life (even if it is no more than to make the best of a bad job) and such general aims as these which are effective and relevant all the time are part of consciousness—we know that we have them and we can see how they influence our talk and behaviour, plans and purposes.

2. Desires

Our life aims can be described as "desires", but they have a more general application and they are more important to most people than those things which we usually call desires. Our desires are desires for specific things which we can usually get in the near future. A man may like good food, drink, women, going to the opera, playing cricket or sitting by the fire with a good book. In most people's lives such desires take second place to their life-aims, and they are not allowed to cause too great an interference in the attempt to bring about the life-aims. For example a man who aims at leading a quiet, undisturbed pleasant life may well control his sexual desire for some particular woman if he thinks that if he did not his normal way of life would be destroyed. It is often the case that such desires have to be passed by because if they were satisfied they would prevent the satisfaction of other desires: if a working man desires to lie late in bed every morning he must not give way to that desire, because if he does he will lose his job and the money that goes with it.

3.   *Habits*

When we desire to do something and then do it we know well enough what has been going on, but there are many things that we do without thinking about them at all.   Most people dress themselves correctly without any thought about what they are doing; many clean their teeth before going to bed without having to "remember" to do so; we switch on the light as we go into a dark room without "desiring light", and so on.   Desires and habits are closely connected, although not all habits originate in desires. The difference can be illustrated by cigarette smoking; some people sometimes desire a cigarette and decide to smoke one, others simply take one and light one without thinking about it at all.

4.   *Instinctive needs*

Instincts often give rise to desires and when they do we become aware of our instinctive needs through the desires to which they give rise.   On the other hand this is not always the case, and we often provide for such needs because we know that we must do so, without having any special desire to do so.   For instance, we all know that it is necessary to eat food and we do this all our life, usually at regular times: we do not always eat because we desire food, we often eat because it is meal-time.   Again, most people instinctively attempt to act in such a way that other people will approve of them and they know, if they think about it, that they like this to happen—and yet it would not be true to say that they acted in this way because they had a desire to win approval.

5. *Principles*

Finally we have principles, and especially moral principles; there are also social principles and conventions.   Principles rarely, if ever, point us to some future goal in the way that our life-aims are directed to some particular achievement.   Principles perform something of the function of a hedge or a fence, or the tracks along which athletes run.   Principles can usually be expressed in rules which are either of the form, "Never do such and such", or else of the form, "Always do such and such".   Examples are: "Tell the truth", "Do not fornicate", "Be polite", "Take off your hat when you meet a lady".

This list of five kinds of things which we have in our minds is not intended to present any special information about the nature of our minds, and it is by no means the only way in which the things in our minds could be grouped.   The nature of consciousness is something which each person must find out for himself by considering what goes on in his own mind, but it is likely that most people will find that some or all of these five kinds of things are represented.   We also need to notice that although there is often a collision or opposition between the things in our minds we usually manage to keep some sort of balance and order between them.   We set aside special times and places to satisfy instinctual necessities (e.g. meal-times); we see to it that our desires do not interfere too much with our life-aims; we try to fulfil both our life-aims and our desires within the limits set by our principles; we regulate our life in order to give ourselves leisure in which to satisfy some of our desires, and so on.   It is also the case that the conflict between things in our minds can set us serious problems: the businessman may find that his life-aim of getting on clashes with his principles of honesty and truth-speaking; desires may interfere with the fulfilling of a life-aim, or they may clash with one's principles. Such problems as these occur and so long as we are aware that such a problem exists it is part of what we know about ourselves.   We call that part of our mind that we know about "consciousness", and it is a most important part of what we are. It is sometimes thought that psychotheraphy tends to give consciousness an unimportant place, and to concentrate attention on the unconscious.   This is not true, but it is true that modern psychotherapy is concerned with many things which we do not know about in the same way that we know about our conscious mind, and these things are spoken of as being "in the unconscious".

Dreams

Most people have dreams at one time or another, and some people say that everyone dreams even though not everyone remembers having dreamed.   We all know what a dream is and we take it for granted that dreams occur, but we do not always realise how very odd dreams are.   One can see that they are very odd by thinking about the way in which we talk about them. When someone begins to describe a dream he says "I dreamt . . ." or "I had a dream about . . .": we take it for granted that to dream is something which we do and so we use active verbs to describe what happened, just as we use an active verb to say, for instance, "I hit someone": but when we dream we do not *do* something, as we do when we hit someone; a dream is not really the result of what we do, it is something which happens to us—it is like being hit rather than hitting, like a brick falling upon one's head.   Very few people can say, "I will now go to sleep and dream about such and such", and even those who can do not make the dream, they simply go to sleep and the dream happens.   We do not make dreams by conscious thought and yet somehow or other a dream is made—the parts of the dream and the images which occur in it are put together in some sort of an arrangement.   Where does the dream come from?

The peculiarity of a dream is that we can neither take responsibility for it ourselves nor point to someone or something else which is responsible for it.   *My* dream is very much my own dream, and I have that particular dream because I am myself—there are no special rooms such that everyone who goes to sleep in a particular one will have the same dream.   The dream seems to have been created by something "inside" me that I know nothing about, it is something for which I am responsible but which does not seem to have been made by anything that I know of in my conscious mind.   Of course we can often find reasons why certain ideas and images should come into our dreams, but we can rarely explain from what we know about ourselves the way those things are arranged —the pattern of the dream.

Dreams are the most easily recognised instances of a class of things which can be described as "odd things". This is an expression which, as we shall use it, has a fairly strict meaning: an "odd thing" is something for which we must regard ourselves as somehow responsible, but which does not seem to fit into what we know about ourselves. A thing is an "odd thing" if we cannot show in what way it is the result of something in our conscious mind, or of some force acting upon us from outside. If dreams were the only "odd things" we might be able to dismiss them as unimportant but there are very many other "odd things", and it is impossible to give a complete picture of a man's behaviour without mentioning some of the odd things which occur in his life. Psychotherapists use the idea of the unconscious in order to talk about "odd things".

Other Odd Things

A clergyman said, "On Wednesday I have to go to So-and-So's funeral"—he meant "wedding". Weddings and funerals are always likely to be connected in a clergyman's mind because they are both special services for which he gets a special fee; nevertheless there were reasons for thinking that this man probably did regard his friend's wedding as more unfortunate than fortunate. Most of us suffer at some time or

another from slips of the tongue, and it does sometimes happen that the thing we actually say has an
obvious meaning quite different from the meaning
of what we intended to say. It can be very embarras-
sing! Slips of the tongue are odd things which we can
talk about by speaking of "the unconscious".

Another rather similar kind of odd thing is the inability to remember some well-known name, of a friend,
a public character or the author of a book for examples.
It is easy to dismiss this as a mere accident, and yet
such things happen very frequently, and it is found
that the idea of the unconscious does help us to understand more about them. Other odd things are
obsessive tunes—melodies which run through our
head for a day or more which we cannot get rid of.
It often happens that we can put words to such tunes
and see why they should have come into our head,
but whether we can see why or not, they are odd
things.

Most people have some occasion to say, "I can't
think why I did that", "I wasn't myself when I said
that", or "I do not know what got into me". A very
good example of the sort of thing which makes people
say things like this is the quarrel between people who are
very fond of one another—often between a courting
couple or husband and wife. On such occasions
neither wants to quarrel, and at the beginning neither
says anything which could not have been said (at some
other time) without causing any trouble, and yet
somehow the antagonism builds up, and the two people
find themselves in the middle of a violent argument
in the course of which they deliberately try to hurt

each other.   The expression "I don't know what got into me" describes this sort of occasion very accurately; it really is as though another "person" takes charge and makes people say and do all sorts of things which they did not mean to say or do.

Very similar to this is the sort of thing which psychotherapists call "excess of affect".   People often find themselves suffering from an emotion which prevents them from thinking or speaking as sensibly as they usually do.   They may be overcome by their anger at something which is said, by their dislike of the person who says something, or by love or affection.   The oddness of such things lies in the power and extent of the affect, not in the existence of anger, dislike or love: the affect is excessive when it plays too large a part in a person's life at the time.   Excess of affect is often connected with political allegiance, so that the mere name "Tory" or "Socialist" may prevent a person from forming any rational opinion about what the person labelled in this way is saying.   At one time this was also true of religious allegiance, but few people nowadays take their religion sufficiently seriously.

Another group of odd things can be described as "moods".   The mark of a mood is that it does not seem to have any very clear cause.   We simply find that our attitude to everything is coloured in the same way—we may see everything through rose-coloured spectacles, or we may take a jaundiced view of the world.   We may just feel that we cannot bear to do any of the things that we know we ought to do, and that there is nothing else that we want to do at all.

These moods often have some obvious cause, but when we think about it we realise that the effect is out of all proportion to the cause. A letter on the breakfast table bringing some trivial piece of bad news—such as that a friend is going to put off a visit, or a member of one's husband's family is coming to stay—may throw one into a mood of sadness for a whole day, and one knows that it is quite unreasonable that it should.

These odd things are things which we all come across at some time or another, and which we have learned to live with. But although we usually manage not to let things of this sort disrupt our lives too much, they remain "odd". We know that they take place, but we cannot really explain why they should, and we let them pass rather than try to get to the bottom of them. In a great many cases this is entirely the right way of treating them, and if there were no other reason for psychotherapy than the existence of such odd things there would probably be no special point in it. Odd things of the kind described above, however, are very closely connected with some forms of mental illness, and the same psychological ideas which help to explain odd things also help the doctor to cope with mental illness.

Mental Illness

The reason why we have called certain things which happen "odd" is that they possess a double character which involves a contradiction. They are "ours", and they are things which we do, and yet at the same

time they do not happen as a result of conscious
purpose and decision. At one and the same time it
is true that we do them and that they happen to us.
They all have a quality about them which can be
indicated most accurately by the idea of "possession".
It really is as though it is not we ourselves but some
alien power within us which is responsible for our
behaviour. This is what actually seems to happen;
that is, it is what it feels like when odd things happen
—the excess emotion, the mood, the deliberate pro-
voking of a quarrel, is something which we never
intended and never consciously caused to happen,
but which nevertheless happened through us. The
idea of the unconscious arises when one carries this
way of thinking about odd things a stage further, and
assumes that there is "something" within us which is
responsible for them, and over which we have no direct
control.

Odd things occur in the life of nearly everyone, and
so they provide a useful approach to the idea of the
unconscious, but the idea was originally elaborated in
connection with the treatment of mental diseases, in
which the idea of "possession" is even more obviously
appropriate than it is in relation to more common odd
things. In the past a great variety of different names
have been used to describe the states of mental disturbance from which people suffer, and the names
have changed from time to time. Today the two
names in most common use are "neurosis" and "psychosis". The odd things of daily life do not usually
cause a great deal of disturbance, but it is obvious
that if they were to become more and more frequent

and of greater strength they would create a serious situation, and we speak of "neurosis" when odd things occur which do cause a real trouble in someone's life. When people suffer from a neurosis they still have a plan of living and still attempt to order their lives according to their conscious plans and intentions, but they find that their attempts are so frustrated by the occurrence of odd things that they are not able to carry out their intentions.   It should be added that they will probably not recognise this themselves, but may well put down their experience of frustration to the cussedness of things around them.   We speak of a "psychosis" when a person's life is disrupted to such an extent that he is no longer able to form and carry out clear and understandable intentions and purposes.

Neurosis

When someone is suffering from a neurosis that person knows what he is trying to do with his life, and he has a more or less clear idea of how he wishes to enter into relationships with people and things, and yet his efforts somehow fail to "come off".   He says silly things when he wants to be particularly sensible, he antagonises the people he wants to impress, things "get on top of him", and he takes attitudes to other people which are quite mistaken.   He may feel that people are somehow against him.   The ideas which people have when they suffer from a neurosis are not absurd, but they are exaggerations of a more reasonable point of view—for instance, the person who is always feeling the need to express thanks out of all proportion to what has been done for him is suffering from a very mild neurosis: his gratitude is not out of place, but it is out of proportion.   A neurotic attitude may not be foolish in itself, but it may be inappropriate to the actual situation.   A person suffering from a neurosis is usually someone to whom one can talk quite sensibly, and if he will try, he is able to get quite a good picture of what is happening to him.   In other words such a person has a conscious mind which is reasonably well organised, but which, at the same time, is not able to cope with all that goes on, and which is liable to lose control over his behaviour.

Psychosis

A neurosis is a disturbance of the mind, which makes it very difficult for a person to cope with life and its problems, and a neurotic person is only too well aware of difficulties with which he is confronted, even if he fails to realise that they have their origin in himself. A psychosis is a disease of the mind, and if a person is suffering from a psychosis there are periods when he is not in touch with the world in which he lives. Psychoses are sometimes associated with a physical degeneration of the brain.

Psychoses are of many different kinds, but they all involve a collapse of the personality in the face of the real or imaginary problems with which a man is confronted.   For example, a psychotic person may not seem to be *a* person at all: his attitude to people and things may shift violently from one extreme to another, so that at one moment he feels surrounded by friends trying to help him, and the next those same people seem to him to be trying to do him down as hard as they can.   Each time one meets him his opinions may be different, and his plans and intentions may vary from day to day or hour to hour.   His inward life may be carried on amid a flood of extraordinary ideas and fantasies which he cannot distinguish from reality.   Other forms of psychosis involve more or less regular changes.   At one time a person is plunged in absolute gloom, he is beset by a sense of misery and despair, and life seems empty and meaningless and everyone and everything seems to be against him. At such times the feeling of depression fills the whole mind, and in this it is different from a depressed "mood", because in a mood of depression we recall other times which were not so "black", we know that there are bright places in the world and we can often take steps to throw it off: when this state is psychotic a person cannot believe that there is anything anywhere except the blackness in which he finds himself.   Such a depressed state (in a psychosis) may be followed by a period of apparent normality, during which the person is able to cope perfectly well with the problems of normal life.   Later the opposite state may occur, and the same person may behave with exaggerated excitement, take no thought for the opinions of others or for convention and appear to have no worries in the world: to such a person the normal limitations on human life seem to have no existence.

In all forms of psychosis the effect made upon other people includes a feeling of uncertainty about who the person suffering from a psychosis is.   Either one does not seem to be able to "get at" the person at all, because his whole life seems to be carried on inside his own mind; or else one never seems to meet more than a small part of him, and seems to meet a different part from one moment to the next; or the character of a person seems to swing from extreme misery to the greatest excitement for very little reason.   Such a person seems to have been split up into bits or driven out of sight by the tribulations of life.

Multiple Personality

There have been a very few well-documented cases of multiple personality.   These cases differ from a psychosis in two important ways.   An individual with multiple personality does not shift with bewildering frequency from one attitude to another, but remains a more or less stable personality for long periods before the personality completely changes.   In other words each personality which takes control is more or less adequate to the demands of life, but now and again hands over control to one of the other personalities. In the two best-known cases only two personalities were originally involved, although a third appeared after treatment had started.   In the more recent case ("Evelyn Lancaster") the two original personalities were known as "Eve White" and "Eve Black". Eve White knew nothing of the other, but Eve Black claimed to know anything she wanted to know about Eve White (thought there was much that she did not bother about!). Eve Black was the personality which disturbed the normal life of Eve White, and on at least two occasions when she got herself into situations that she could not control she simply "disappeared" and left Eve White to take control.

The Ego

Simple "odd things" which we all come across, like dreams and slips of the tongue, neuroses and psychoses have one thing in common—they all involve behaviour which people do not deliberately plan, which they do not intend and for which they are not responsible in the way in which they are responsible for the normal ordering of their lives.   In order to talk about things like this one needs to be able to distinguish between the things which a person does deliberately and intention- ally and those which, as it seems, happen through a person. In order to do this we speak of the "ego" when we are thinking about deliberate and conscious action. In other words the ego controls the life of a normal person except when "odd things" occur, and we speak of the ego as "the centre of consciousness". It is, perhaps, more correct to think of the ego as a group of conscious psychic elements which are so bound together that they usually co-operate with each other.   When we think of the ego like this we can then think of the odd things as the result of interference with the work of the ego by other psychic elements which we do not know about, but which influence our minds.

Simple odd things occur in the life of a person who

has a relatively developed ego, and they do not cause any very great disturbance in his life. The neurotic person has a relatively weak ego, and although it normally keeps control of the person's life it is subjected to great interference by other psychic forces which prevent it from dealing adequately with the problems of living. Psychosis affects the ego itself. The ego may give up the attempt to control life in the real world and retire into a world of dreams, or it may be completely overthrown, from time to time by some other force (or forces) which takes control for a greater or longer period. Except when the ego is in control the psychotic person does not seem to be complete at all, but in the rare case of multiple personality the separate sources of control all seem to be reasonably well-organised as "egos" in themselves, and that is why each one behaves like a relatively normal person.

The Unconscious

"The unconscious" is the name given to the "container" of the "somethings" which are able to interfere with the normal conscious directions of life. Since it is found convenient to talk as though these unknown things in an individual can take control, it is also convenient to picture those things as somehow existing in the individual. We say that they are "unconscious" or that they are "in the unconscious". Thus, for example, if we mean to speak kindly and friendlily to someone and a hard and bitter phrase slips out, we may say that we had an unconscious desire to hurt and distress that person, even though we thought we felt entirely amicable towards him.

It is very important, and sometimes difficult, to remember that if something is unconscious we really do not know anything about it. When, for example, we claim that a slip of the tongue reveals an attitude to someone else which we do not know about, we do not expect that we shall then realise that we do take that attitude to them. Even people who are used to using psychological terms sometimes make this mistake, and it is very irritating when they do. When, for instance, an unkind phrase slips out one might say to the person who let it slip, "It looks as though you have an unconscious dislike of that man"; if he replies, "Not at all, I admire him tremendously, and regard him as the most delightful person imaginable", that shows that he has not the least real idea of what it means to say that something is unconscious. The difficulty is that there are degrees of unconsciousness, and there are times when an odd thing does bring home to us the existence of an attitude or idea which we did not realise we had before: this may happen but there is no reason why it should, and when we think that we can see how an odd thing reveals some unconscious attitude or idea we do not expect the person concerned to know any more about it than we who are watching him can see.

The unconscious is only known by the way in which it influences a person's life, and when we talk about the unconscious we are talking about the odd things to which we have referred above—the things which do not "fit" into what we know of ourselves. It is not

really correct to say that there are things "in the
unconscious" because if there are we can never know
them, nor examine them, as we can examine the
brain or an amoeba under the microscope.   What we
have really done is to form a picture in our minds
which helps us to talk about odd things.   In fact it
is found that this picture is extremely helpful in a great
many ways, and this is the reason why we are justified
in using it.   It is a fact that things happen in our
lives which we cannot attribute to outside influence,
but for which we do not feel responsible, in the sense
of having decided, intended or chosen to do them,
and this is just as much a fact about human nature
as the fact that we sometimes know just how and why
we came to do something.   Any full account of
human living must take this into account, and the idea
of the unconscious is found to be a most helpful and
valuable way of doing so.

The Psyche

So far we have been using the expression "the mind"
in a very loose way: we should keep the word "mind"
to refer to our mental selves as we know ourselves by
introspection.   In other words "mind" means consciousness.   As we have just said this is all that we
actually know about ourselves, and the unconscious
is simply a picture which helps us to talk about the
odd things which happen in our lives.   It is very
natural that in forming our picture of the unconscious
we should picture it as more of the same sort of things
that go to make up our "minds", and to imagine a

totality which is made up of consciousness and the unconscious.　When we do this we use the word "psyche" to refer to the whole lot.　Thus the psyche is the idea of a total inner world which is made up of both conscious and unconscious elements.

Although we cannot know for certain that the unconscious part of the psyche (or "the unconscious psyche") is the same sort of thing as the conscious part (the mind) we do know that it has the same sort of effect on our behaviour as the conscious part.　If we hate someone we are likely to say something nasty to him, and if we hate someone unconsciously we may say something nasty by accident: the difference is that we know what we are doing in the first instance, we do not in the second.　The fact that consciousness and the unconscious do influence us in very much the same ways is a good reason for thinking of them as two parts of one thing—the thing we call "the psyche."

The psyche is a living organism constantly developing, and this is equally true of each of its two parts—consciousness and the unconscious.　We can take note of the changes which go on in consciousness, and say, for instance, "I wouldn't have said that a few years ago", or, "I should never have behaved like that last year", or, "My ideas have developed a lot since then": if we keep a diary, or a very close watch on our thoughts we can look back and see how our minds have changed and developed over a period of time. We think of the unconscious as changing and developing in much the same way, except that we have no means of observing the actual process of change: what happens is that the odd things which result from the interference of our lives by unconscious elements take different forms from time to time, indicating that the unconscious itself has changed.

Chapter IV: HOW THE PSYCHE FUNCTIONS

A Picture of the Psyche

WE do not know what the unconscious is like, so that any picture that we make of the psyche is only a convenient way of thinking about it. That means that no picture is the one, correct picture, and the picture which we describe here is only one of many ways of thinking about the psyche.

One is to imagine a cylinder full of water, dropping down like a shaft out of sight. A very small section at the top of the cylinder is illuminated, and one can see clearly the things that float in it. As one looks deeper so one's vision becomes less clear, and the greater part of the contents of the cylinder are completely invisible. There is considerable movement in the part that is illuminated, and one can see how some things slowly sink out of sight while others rise up out of the depths.

The top, lighted section represents the conscious mind, and the things which can be seen in it represent all those thoughts, ideas, desires and so on that we know about. These things are seen to form a kind of pattern: a larger number of them are grouped together to form a fairly dense mass. This mass represents "ego-consciousness", the dominant ideas and characteristics of one's personality. Other things are loosely connected with this central mass, and others have hardly any connection with it at all. It is those things which are least connected with the central mass that tend to sink out of sight. The deep part of the cylinder in which we can see nothing represents the unconscious.

The Threshold of Consciousness

The picture includes a kind of half-way area, between the full light of consciousness and the unconscious. This is the area in which vision is becoming obscured, but in which things can still be seen as moving shapes. In actual living this represents the fact that there are many things "at the back of our minds" which we can easily become aware of if we turn our attention to them, but which we more often ignore.

We speak of the "threshold of consciousness" to indicate this area in between consciousness and the unconscious: those things which are "above the threshold" are fully conscious, and play their part in our lives almost continually, those which are "below the threshold" are unconscious, and can only influence our lives in devious ways. The things below the threshold are said to be "subliminal", which simply means "below the threshold".

Examples of subliminal things can be given fairly easily. At any moment we receive sense-impressions from our external environment, but there is a great deal to which we do not turn our attention. We may, for instance, not notice where the chairs in a room are until we come to sit down—and then we find that we know where to sit. We may remember some feature of a room after we have left it, even though we do not remember noticing that feature when we were in the room. We may have forgotten the look of a street which we once knew very well, and yet recall it in detail if we happen to return to it. We may have bits of knowledge "tucked away" in the back of our minds which we are not called upon to use, but which we can "bring out" unexpectedly if occasion should arise. These subliminal things are not normally "there" in consciousness, but they are in no way lost, and can be "fished up" if they are wanted.

Things which are subliminal in this way pass in and out of consciousness, that is they are able to move across the threshold of consciousness. This is fairly easy to understand. It is not quite so easy to understand how the threshold of consciousness can move. In the picture this simply means that sometimes the lighted area of the top section becomes larger and at other times smaller, but it can also mean that the light can move away from the main group which represents the ego-centre of consciousness to some other part of the cylinder. The enlarging and decreasing of the lighted area is connected with "concentration": to concentrate is to direct our attention to one or two specially selected ideas or images in our minds, and to ignore all the rest. This means that very much more is subliminal than is usually the case, and we can express this by saying that the threshold of conscious-ness has been raised. For instance, if one is studying very hard the noise of a bell which one would normally notice may not "get through" at all, and one may not know that it has rung.   On the other hand, when one's mind is relaxed or drifting the threshold of consciousness is lowered, and thoughts and images may come into it (out of the unconscious) which one had not been aware of before.   The shifting of the light from the central part of consciousness represents the experience that sometimes accompanies an over-powering emotion such as fear or love.   At such times the normal attitudes, principles and habits may be completely forgotten and one is guided by powers from within which would normally be controlled. This is, in effect, a lowering of the threshold, whereby unconscious elements are able to play a greater part than usual in one's life.

The Unconscious

As we have said, the dark, lower part of the cylinder represents the unconscious, and there are one or two things which must be remembered about it.   It is dark, which means that we do not know what is in it, but at the same time the things in the unconscious are able to affect consciousness.   They do this in two main ways.   First of all they cause us to have ideas, thoughts, moods and images in our conscious minds, and this is both an advantage and a disadvantage.   It is an advantage because we could never develop our conscious minds at all if we did not receive new things from the unconscious.   It is a disadvantage because these things sometimes interfere unduly with our conscious thinking and planning.   The things in the unconscious can also sometimes take control of the body and influence our physical behaviour—and in particular our speech.

So far we have simply thought of the unconscious as a dark lump lying beneath consciousness, but in the course of their work psychotherapists have found it necessary to picture the unconscious as a changing structured arrangement of parts, with its own divisions and organisation.

What we have said in this chapter is more or less generally accepted by all psychotherapists, but when one begins to discuss the structure of the unconscious the divisions between the psychotherapeutic schools begin to be important.   They are mainly divided by the way in which they picture the internal arrangement of the unconscious psyche.   In the remainder of this chapter we shall continue to explain certain ideas which are common to all schools.

Repression

There is general agreement that many of the things in the unconscious have become unconscious as a result of repression, and the idea of repression is used in all forms of psychotherapy.   This means that there are some things in the unconscious which have at one time or another been conscious, and "repression" is the word used to indicate that this has happened. Repression is very closely connected with forgetting.

Someone once pointed out that the ability to forget is quite as valuable and remarkable as the ability to remember. It is always nice to be able to remember something, but if we were to remember every single thing that had ever happened to us there would simply be no room in our minds at all. We should be smothered by our memories. The process of forgetting is represented in our picture when a thing falls into the darkness, out of the light of consciousness: that is when it becomes subliminal. We must say that such things are subliminal and not that they have gone out of our minds, because it is a well-known fact that long-forgotten memories can be revived under the influence of the right stimulus: although we may have forgotten something there is an important sense in which it is still "there" in our psyche, and this is what we mean by saying that it is unconscious.

The difference between forgetting and repression is largely a matter of degree, and it is marked by the difficulty of bringing something back to consciousness at the appropriate time. Something which has merely been forgotten can usually be recovered if it would be useful, but a thing which has been repressed can only be brought back into consciousness after great effort: much psychological analysis is concerned with the recovery of repressed things. Whereas we may think of forgotten things as things which have sunk gently out of consciousness it is as though repressed things have had a great weight attached to them, to ensure that they shall not float up again.

Why should some things be repressed? The answer is that we repress those things which we feel cannot be accepted within the central organisation of consciousness. For examples, if there is a dominant desire in consciousness, then we shall tend to repress a principle which lays it down that such a desire should not be fulfilled: if a certain principle is an important feature of consciousness, then we shall repress a desire which could only be fulfilled at the expense of that principle. We also repress those things which destroy our idea of what we are. For example, if someone has done a mean and cowardly thing he has to make a choice: either he must admit that he is the sort of person who is liable to do this sort of thing, or else he must put the fact that he has done it entirely out of mind—that is, he must repress the memory of it. If he admits that he is the sort of person who might do such a thing he cannot go on thinking of himself as a brave man, as, we must assume, he did before. The things which we repress, are things which would endanger our idea of ourselves if we remembered them—either by proving that we are not the sort of person that we like to think we are, or else by tending to lead us to do things which do not fit in with our idea of ourselves. Recently the late Archbishop of Canterbury remarked about sexual sins: "We must tell our people that they should not do these things, nor desire to do them", and this was a recommendation that people should not merely control but also repress their sexual desires—that is thrust them out from their conscious minds. Repression is the way in which we evade moral problems: instead of admitting that there is a clash between different aspects of our nature, and seeking to cope with it we simply reject one side in favour of the other.

It is usual to speak of repression as though it were something that is always bad, but this is not the whole truth. Although there is usually something undesirable about repression, it has its part to play in the development of the individual. The things which are repressed are things which are some kind of threat to the stability of consciousness. For example, one may repress a painful memory of some foolish or irresponsible act, because if one were to remember it one would lose confidence in oneself, and be unable to cope with one's work and duties: or one may repress a bad act because remembering it would make it almost impossible for one to develop the better side of one's character. Sometimes repression of things like this is absolutely essential if a person is to grow and mature—although it may become equally essential to remember what had been repressed when growth has progressed sufficiently. Repression plays a specially important part in the early stages of adult life, when the most important thing for the young person to do is to develop an organised and stable ego-consciousness with which to confront other people and the world. Yet when all this has been said it is still true that repression is more undesirable than it is a good thing, and there are two main reasons why.

The first reason why repression is more bad than good is that it means losing some part of oneself. When we wholly forget something we have thought or done, or something which has happened to us it is not merely a matter of forgetting that thing, we also refuse to see that we are the sort of person capable of behaving in the way that we did. If a memory is

repressed it is because that memory is in some way
bound up with a tendency within us which we prefer
to think we do not have, and from this point of view
repression means the loss of something that belongs
to us, and with which the ego must eventually come
to terms. To say this, that the ego must come to
terms with the repressed aspect of our nature, is to
introduce the idea of "ought", and it is always dangerous to do this in connection with psychology. It may
be that there are things which would be so destructive
to a man's character if he did not repress them that
it is much better that they should remain repressed;
and it is certain that there are right times for everything, so that it may well be that it is better not to
recover a repressed memory at some particular time.
If, for example, a person represses a very large number
of things, and still manages to live a full, useful and
satisfactory life it would probably be wrong to say
that he ought to come to terms with the things which
he has repressed. The idea that we "ought" to
become aware of repressed memories comes from the
feeling that the development of the whole of our
nature is a good thing, and if this is indeed the case it
follows that repression is a bad thing, because it makes
it impossible for the repressed aspects of our nature
to be included in our organised consciousness.

The other reason why repression is liable to be a bad
thing is that it does not do what we should like it to
do. If we repress the memory of some occasion
when we behaved in a thoroughly selfish and unpleasant way we are able to think of ourselves and
behave as though we were unselfish and pleasant, but

this does not alter the true facts.   If we did on some occasion act selfishly this was because there are selfish elements in our characters, and by repressing the memory we have merely refused to admit this—we have not "got rid" of the selfish elements.   In other words, although the result of repression may be that we do not know about a particular tendency within us, that tendency is still there, and it is liable to interfere with our conscious aims.   This is often very marked in relation to selfishness, for example, in the case of a person who consciously works very hard for other people "never thinking of herself", and then has a complete breakdown which forces others to start looking after her.   Again there are people who arrange things in such a way that it is obvious to everyone else that they have come well out of it, and who yet imagine that all they have done was for the most altruistic and high-minded motives imaginable.   Repressed tendencies are able to cause all kinds of peculiar distortions in our behaviour, just because we do not know about them: when we realise that we have tendencies of a particular kind we can do something about trying to control them; but so long as they remain unconscious we can exercise no control over them whatsoever.

It should be kept very clearly in mind that we do not repress things in the way that we neglect a piece of work which we know we ought to do, for example. Repression is not something which we do, but something which happens to us.   If we really try to forget something we are rarely successful; things are repressed without any deliberate and conscious choice on our part.   Thus to say that "we repress" something is not strictly correct, it is rather that something is repressed. As we have said repression is a psychic means of avoiding conflict between our conscious character and other tendencies within us, and this means that if by some means we are able to recall something which we have repressed this does not make things easier for us—it usually confronts us with conflicts and problems which we had previously avoided.   It is important to remember this when speaking about psychological analysis.   It is a great mistake to suppose that this makes things easier—what it does is to make a person more aware of his total character and (potentially) more able to take responsibility for all that he does. The recovery of repressed memories and ideas should stop many things going on which the individual is unable to control, but it also sets him a hard task in coming to terms with the recovered memories and tendencies within him.

Devaluation

Repression is one way of avoiding conflicts but there are also other ways, and they could all be grouped together under the term "devaluation".   We may avoid an internal conflict by refusing to give full value to this or that element of the conflict.   "Devaluation" of this kind is brought about by repressing the feeling-tone and the psychic energy of an element, so that it is quite possible for people to devalue elements of their characters without repressing the element itself, and this seems to be an important fact. Unfortunately very little has been said about it in most works on psychology and it has not received the attention it deserves. Much is said about repression, and it is clear that devaluation has a very similar result, but in a different way.

When one represses something one does not know about it at all: if a tendency opposed to one's conscious aims is repressed then the problem is simply removed. On the other hand one can get rid of a problem by devaluing the opposing tendency, even though one does not cease to be aware that it is present. This can be instanced in relation to sex. Most people have now learnt how it comes about that a person with strong, puritan views about sex often tends to suspect sexual immorality in others, and even to go out of his or her way to find evidence of it. This is a classic example of repression—such a person has such strong views about the badness or wrongness of sex that he cannot admit to having sexual instincts and tendencies, so that they get repressed: since they cannot express themselves in the natural way as sexual desires they interfere with consciousness in a round-about way by causing excessive concern about the sexual behaviour of others. Someone with equally strong views about immorality may cope with the problem in rather a different way. He may be quite ready to admit that he has sexual instincts and desires which are not entirely confined to a marriage relation-ship, but he may find that they never cause him any serious problem or difficulty. Such a man has not repressed his sex instincts since he is aware of them, but he has succeeded in evading the problem which they might present him by taking away from them their psychic strength (i.e psychic energy). We do not devalue in this kind of way by conscious choice, any more than we deliberately repress a thing; like repression it is simply something which happens.

Another instance of devaluation can be given in connection with religious faith. The religious fanatic has clearly repressed his doubts, and many others with "simple faith" are in the same state. There are those, however, who do not deny that their belief rests upon something less than certain knowledge, but who manage to admit to real doubts without letting those doubts become a serious problem. In many ways devaluation appears to be a thoroughly good thing—it serves the main purpose of repression without involving one in the more obvious dangers of repression. At the same time it seems to imply a serious loss. If one has instincts, or doubts, this is a real and important fact about oneself which must result in a real tension and conflict; if one devalues these things one evades the tension but one also loses the energy which is connected with what has been devalued. This devaluation of things in the psyche is something which most people can investigate for themselves in their own lives, and it is clearly a very important feature in the lives of many people.

Rationalisation

When something is repressed it still influences conscious life. Repressed elements are unconscious and they express themselves in the "odd things" of which we have already spoken. It may appear strange that this can go on happening without a person's becoming aware that his life is being influenced by things which he knows nothing about, but this is certainly what happens, and people show the most extraordinary ability to remain unaware of odd things which are obvious to other people. In a sense it is all part of repression, because the effect of repression is to hide things away from conscious knowledge. Two simple ways in which we hide the odd things from ourselves are by further repression and devaluation: by repression we simply put the odd incident out of our minds, and by devaluation we refuse to admit that it has any real importance. For example, suppose that we dislike someone but do not admit to ourselves that we dislike that person (i.e. suppose we repress our dislike of him), and suppose that dislike expresses itself by causing us to forget to post a letter to him. It is very easy to forget that we made this mistake, even after we have found the letter and posted it. This is to conceal the odd thing by further repression. If the odd things are slips of the tongue, or strange ideas it is very easy to tell ourselves that they have no importance or significance whatsoever, and if we do this we conceal them by devaluing them. However, the most usual way of hiding odd things from ourselves is by "rationalisation", which means telling ourselves that they were not really odd at all.

An elderly woman climbs a fairly steep path with a group of younger people. She not only wishes to show them that she has no trouble in walking up the path, she is convinced in her own mind that she is just as capable of getting up as the others, and quite sure that she does not need to take more rests than they do. Some way up she stops and turns round to look back. Why has she stopped? it is quite obvious to the on-looker that she has stopped in order to recover her breath before going on with the climb, but if she were to think this herself it would not fit in with her cer-tainty that she could manage as well as everyone else. *She* knows perfectly well that she has stopped in order to admire the view, which is particularly delightful at this spot. This is rationalisation, and like repression and devaluation it is something that happens to us, not something that we do. The elderly lady did not "think up" an excuse for stopping, she really did say to herself "I really must look at the view from this point", and she really did believe that this was the reason why she stopped. For her there was no odd thing, nothing which could suggest to her that she was mistaken in thinking that she was as capable of climbing the hill as anyone else.

Another woman had been brought up with some-what excessive ideas about modesty, in particular about being seen naked. As she grew up she had corrected these ideas (as she imagined) and realised that there were certain situations when modesty of this sort was not a good thing. When, however, she and her husband made love with the light on she always found that it caused her some kind of distress—it got in her eyes, or it was too bright or something like that—so that it had to be turned out. Because she planned to be open and to make love in the light the turning out of the light was an odd thing which did not fit in with her conscious intention, but it did not appear to her to be odd because she always had an explanation for it, which had nothing to do with her repressed modesty. Perhaps it should be added that there is nothing specially "odd" about choosing to make love either with the light on or in the dark, the "oddness" of which we are speaking arises when one intends one thing and does the other. In most instances of rationalisation the reason which we find in order to explain the odd thing which happens is a good one which really does make sense, but whether it is or not it always takes us in. It sometimes takes other people in as well, but at other times it is clear to others that the reason which we give is not the right one.

From the point of view of the observer a common mark of rationalisation is the multiplication of different reasons for the same thing. Suppose one notices that someone always crosses the road at a particular point, although it is an inconvenient place to cross. If one asks about this on one occasion and is told that it was in order to post a letter in the pillar box on the other side one accepts the explanation, but if on another day the person says "let's cross over, it's sunnier over there", and on yet another day "I just want to cross over to see how the flowers are getting on in Mr. Brown's garden", and later on "There's Mrs. Green coming, I don't want to waste time talking to her, let's cross over"—then one begins to think that there is something odd about it, and one may remember that if one did not cross at that point one would pass a garden in which there was a large dog which barked at passers-by. Again someone may give a reason for something and his reason may sound a good one, but then one points out to him that it is not really a good one—immediately he offers a completely different reason for the same thing, and when this is shown to be mistaken he produces yet another reason: and so it goes on.

The reason for this multiplicity of explanations is that when we rationalise we are not able to give the real reason for our act or attitude, because it is unconscious, and if we are not giving the real reason it does not really matter what other reason we give—all are as good (or as bad) as each other, and we are quite content to try them out one after the other: anything, in fact, is better than discovering the true reason. Rationalisation, of course, is like straightforward deceit when we are at pains to prevent someone else from finding out our real reason, but it differs from this in that it is ourselves who are deceived— though *we* do not deceive anybody, not even ourselves, it is rather that we are deceived. We really think that the reasons we give are the right ones, and so we are able to avoid noticing that odd things take place.

Projection

Projection is also a means whereby we hide from ourselves the unconscious cause of odd things. By rationalising odd things we are able to admit that we are responsible for them, and also to hide the thing which causes them; by projection we become aware of the unconscious source of odd things, but hide the fact that it is in ourselves. For instance, suppose a man who thinks of himself as good-natured and tolerant has a repressed and unconscious hatred for someone else. When a quarrel flares up between them it is an odd thing, and the man may either rationalise it or project his unconscious hatred. If he rationalises it he will admit that he caused the quarrel but explain it away as the result of a hard day's work, or of some source of irritation not connected with the other man: that is, he accepts responsibility while hiding the unconscious cause. If he projects his hatred he will claim that the other person started the quarrel, and that he did so because of his dislike of the first man. The man with unconscious hatred thinks that the hatred comes from the other man.

The prudish person who finds sexual immorality everywhere is also projecting. He or she denies the strength of his own tendency to sexual immorality, but makes the assumption that other people (often the young) are obsessed by their sex instincts—he sees in others what he refuses to see in himself. A more complicated form of projection occurs when people "fall in love" and seem to see the person with whom they are in love through a kind of shining cloud. What has happened is that an idealised idea of what a woman (or a man) should be exists in the mind of the young man (or woman) and he projects this upon the actual woman—that is, he does not see her as she really is, but as an embodiment of his own ideal. Such a projection makes it impossible for a man to see what the woman is really like, and it is very often most irritating to the person on whom the projection is made. In this instance it is not so much an unconscious tendency which has been projected as a complicated idea in one's mind of which one is not fully conscious. When we project we become aware of things which are in our own unconscious, but we become aware of them as it were in the wrong place. It is very like a magic lantern which projects an image on to a screen some distance away—the person or thing upon whom we project unconscious elements is used as a screen.

Projection causes us to make wrong judgements about the source of odd things, and also about the character of people and things with whom we have to do, but it must not be supposed that projection is merely a matter of what we think about other people. Projection is able to have remarkably powerful effects upon the person on whom it is made. First it should be realised that we rarely project something on to someone else unless there is some reason for doing so. For example, if John Smith has an unconscious hatred for Peter Brown he is not likely to project that hatred (that is, to think that Peter Brown hates him) if Peter Brown is absolutely free of all (conscious or unconscious) dislike of him. The act of projecting tends to arouse the dormant dislike in Peter Brown, so that as a result of the projection Peter Brown does actually behave in a more unpleasant way towards John Smith than he would otherwise have done. Again, if one has repressed one's more severe and "schoolmistressy" attitudes and projects them on to someone else, then that other person probably will speak to one

in a schoolmistressy way.   These effects of projection are obviously of great importance in personal
relationships, and a lot of misunderstandings can be
avoided by those who are aware of the power which
projection can have in constellating in the other person
characteristics which would play a very minor rôle if
it were not for projection.   For example, if one has
treated someone unjustly but refuses to admit it, then
one projects upon him a sense of being badly treated,
and he acts accordingly, but if one can bring oneself
to admit the truth there is no projection, and the
person who has been badly treated is likely to behave
in a much more understanding way (if he is an understanding person to begin with!).

Complexes

Psychic elements do not exist in isolation, either in
consciousness or in the unconscious.   For example,
we do not often have a single, simple attitude to another
person: we find this person admirable but dull, another
person fascinating and at the same time someone of
whom we disapprove and so on.   We may take a
complex attitude to our job, it may be to us a necessary
nuisance, an interesting job, hard work and an escape
from tensions at home—and it may be all these things
at the same time.   "Being in love", friendship, rivalry
and many other common relationships between people
are extremely complicated, and they are made up of
a number of elements which are bound together to
form a whole.   This tendency for psychic elements
to become bound together accounts for the fact, for

instance, that we find it difficult to disapprove of someone we like very much, or to like someone of whom we disapprove—even though the person we like may do things of which we would normally disapprove, and the person of whom we disapprove may be very likeable.

Consciousness itself is really a large complex, and our conscious character is formed from an immense number of elements, many of them grouped together in subsidiary complexes. The more stable a person is the more closely bound together are the elements which form his consciousness, and the less united they are the more likely he is to behave in inconsistent ways. There are many people whose conscious character seems to consist of one or two complexes which have little relationship to each other: such people may be said to be "one person at work, and another in his own home", or it may be said "He is a different person again when he gets with a group of his special cronies". On the whole there is something which strikes us as "reasonable" in the grouping of elements in consciousness, and complexes are usually formed for sound reasons, but even in consciousness it often happens that complexes tend to cause errors of judgement. For example, if someone has been extremely badly treated by a person with a beard, he may connect the idea of an untrustworthy person with the idea of a beard, and he may tend to suspect people with beards. Normally this will be no more than a tendency, and it will soon be corrected in particular cases, but certain complexes of this sort cause widespread chaos—for example, the complex connected with Jews in Christian Europe (rooted in the condemnation of the Jews for crucifying Jesus), or the complex attitude of white-skinned races to black-skinned people which is connected with the contrast between light and darkness.

If conscious complexes are sometimes less than reasonable it need cause no surprise that complexes in the unconscious should be largely unreasonable. It seems that psychic elements tend to become connected together, and if they are unconscious they may be bound together for reasons which seem to be wholly trivial. Unconscious connections between psychic elements may depend upon similarity of sound or appearance, the fact that two things occurred at the same time, a pun and so on. What happens when elements are grouped together like this is that the attitude and energy which belongs to one is shared with the other, and so long as the whole thing is unconscious we can do very little to overcome this. If, for example, one has repressed the fact that a man with a beard has let one down badly, then one will have no way of discovering why it is that one never manages to get on with people who wear beards, and the expectation that people with certain names will behave in appropriate ways is largely due to unconscious complexes formed from our previous experience of people with those names (both in real life, in literature and at the cinema).

The tendency for unconscious elements to form into complexes means that when something is repressed it gets attached to things already in the unconscious, and this influences both the repressed element and the thing to which it becomes attached. For example, suppose a fairly trivial misdemeanour is repressed, it may well become bound up in the unconscious with far more serious tendencies to evil, and so influence us (through "odd things") far more devastatingly than it would have done otherwise. Again, if we repress something as evil it may get connected with something rising out of the unconscious which should become conscious, and if it does it will tend to act as a "sinker" which prevents that thing from becoming conscious. For example, someone who has had an unhappy and unfortunate love affair may repress the worst features of it, and they may then become bound up with a later tendency to fall in love with someone else, and make this impossible. There will be more to be said about complexes in later chapters.

SUMMARY

The main psychic activities explained in this chapter are—

Repression—the complete failure to recollect certain past events, and the complete ignorance of the existence of certain aspects of our character.

Devaluation—the effective neutralisation of some aspect of our character by removing psychic energy from it.

Rationalisation—the conviction that one knows why one did something when in fact the reason was quite different.

Projection—attributing our own unconscious tendencies to other people.

It is necessary to remember that all these things are things that happen, and not things that we choose to do.   We cannot purposely repress a thing, because we have to know about it to do this, and if we know about it, it is not repressed.   If a thing is repressed we simply do not know it.   In order to purposely devalue something we should have to be aware of its strength, but if it is devalued we simply do not realise it is an important tendency within us.   When we project we have no idea that we are doing so, and think that the other person is responsible for all that is going on.   It seems that it must be true that we are in some way "responsible" for these things, but we are not responsible for them in the way that we are responsible for our conscious choice and decisions—these things simply happen, and the most that can be said is that when they happen to us they do so because we are the people that we are.   It is some comfort to remember that they happen to everyone!

Chapter V: THE COLLECTIVE UNCONSCIOUS

Divisions of the Psyche

ALL psychotherapists think of the psyche as having the two parts of which we have spoken—consciousness and the unconscious, and there cannot be any very serious differences of opinion about what is found in consciousness, because this is known to anyone who practises a little introspection. Different schools of psychotherapy, however, vary a great deal in their approach to the way in which the rest of the psyche is thought of. As we have seen Freudians think in terms of Id, Sub-conscious, Ego and Superego, and this is one way of dividing the contents of the psyche into groups. In this chapter we shall describe the Jungian picture of the psyche, and according to Jung the important groupings of psychic contents are Consciousness, the Personal Unconscious and the Collective Unconscious. This way of dividing the psyche into groups was introduced by Jung, and forms one of the most important distinguishing features of his teaching. The idea of the Personal Unconscious is easier to understand than that of the Collective Unconscious.

The Personal Unconscious

The account given in the last chapter of what might
be called the "top layer" of the unconscious would
probably be accepted by the majority of psychotherapists.   It is generally agreed that there are in
the unconscious things which have as it were "fallen
out" of consciousness—memories that we have forgotten, things that we have seen or heard without taking
proper notice of them, habits and tendencies of one
sort or another.   It is also generally agreed that there
are things which have been repressed, and that
these things tend to group together to form unconscious complexes.   There might not be quite so much
agreement about a further group of things which Jung
says are in the top layer of the unconscious.   These are
things which have never been conscious, but which
are on the way to becoming conscious.

The idea that there are things which start in the
depths of the unconscious and slowly work their way
up into consciousness may seem, at first sight, to be
slightly curious, but it accords very well with our
everyday experience.   Anyone who has had anything
to do with the personal development of another
person (whether he be a psychotherapist, priest or
university tutor, for examples) soon realises that it is
not enough to tell that person something, he must be
ready to receive and accept it before it can mean anything to him at all.   It is a common (and yet always
surprising) experience to have repeatedly pointed
something out to a person over a period of weeks or

months or years, and then to hear him suddenly saying exactly the same thing in a tone of great surprise, as a new truth which he has just discovered. The same thing, of course, is true of the education of children; a child can only be taught certain things at any given time, and if one tries to teach him things which he is not ready to learn he just does not receive them—and it is very unfortunate when a child is not taught the things which he is ready to learn.   In other words "underneath" our conscious mind there is continual development going on, and ideas and attitudes are preparing in the unconscious for long periods before they actually enter into consciousness. According to Jung such unconscious psychic elements are also in the "top layer" of consciousness, and they tend to form complexes with the other elements in that layer.   This is why repression can often prevent further development, when something "on the way up" gets bound up in a complex with something which has been repressed.

It is clear that the things in the top layer of the unconscious are closely connected with the nature of a man's conscious personality.   We do not repress everything unpleasant, but only those things which are a special danger to us.   A man who sets out to keep a very strict moral code is likely to repress the tendencies within him which are liable to conflict with that code; the libertine will repress the moral tendencies which oppose his licentiousness; the man who prides himself on his reasonableness represses his irrational tendencies; the man who aims to be a strong man will repress his weaker characteristics.   The repressed elements are repressed because they have some special connection with those elements which are conscious, and the most usual connection is that of standing in opposition to the conscious elements. Thus it can be said that the top layer of the unconscious in any particular person is what it is largely because he is the (conscious) person that he is. In other words the top layer of the unconscious is bound up with the personal characteristics of an individual, and for this reason Jung calls it the "Personal Unconscious": its contents and the way they are grouped are different in each individual.

Manifestations of the Collective Unconscious

We have suggested that we can think of psychic elements rising up through the unconscious until they eventually enter consciousness. When we think in this way it is natural that we should ask where they come from, and the answer must be that they come from some deeper level of the unconscious. It is, however, always to be remembered that when we speak in this way about "levels" within the unconscious we are using a model, we do not know anything about what the unconscious is in itself, and all we can do is to think in terms of models which help us to talk about what actually goes on. We may think of a "deeper layer" of the unconscious, and we call this deeper layer the "Collective Unconscious", but what we are really concerned with are those things happening in our lives which we regard as manifestations of the collective unconscious.

The elements in the collective unconscious manifest themselves in the same way as other unconscious elements, that is by causing ideas, attitudes and behaviour which do not fit in with the normal life of the person concerned; but the manifestations of the collective unconscious are rather different from those of the personal unconscious.   Manifestations of the collective unconscious are, in a way, more odd than the effects of other unconscious elements, and they often have an outrè quality about them.   The result of their greater oddness is that there is more resistance to them in the conscious psyche, so that they are less likely to crop up in the course of actual living than are the effects of other unconscious things: they turn up only when one is relaxed and off guard in dreams or day-dreams, or in special circumstances—and also in serious cases of mental disturbance.

Manifestations of the collective unconscious are liable to be "larger than life".   It may be odd that an indifferently efficient office boy should dream of becoming the manager of the department but there is nothing extraordinary about it so long as it remains little more than a dream or reverie.   Fantasies about the possible but improbable are common enough and occur in most peoples lives.   On the other hand day-dreams which include ideas of having supreme power in the universe, and having the power of life and death in relation to other men and women are rather less normal, and verge towards actual insanity.   The dream of Joseph described in the Old Testament in which the sun and the moon and the stars bowed down before him has this larger than life quality, and so have dreams or fantasies in which one is seeking for some unthinkable treasure, or some new knowledge which will solve all the problems of the world.   Probably such things as these crop up at some time in some way or another in the lives of most people, but most of us are able to detect the fantastic element in them, and to refuse to take them seriously.   Psychotherapists, on the other hand, encounter instances in which ideas such as these have got such a grip on a person that either he is unable to dismiss them even when he is aware of their foolishness, or else he becomes so obsessed by them that he loses all contact with reality.

Beside the "larger than life" quality, those things which are called manifestations of the collective unconscious are also marked by the fact that they appear to crop up again and again in human history.   It is largely due to Jung that psychotherapists have searched among ancient writings and the systems of ancient religions for parallels to the things they encounter in their consulting-rooms.   What has been found is that the majority of those dreams and fantasies which have a larger than life quality, and which strike the patient as being of great importance include ideas and images which are also found in mythology and religion.   It is not always possible to prove that there has been no previous knowledge of the older ideas in the mind of the patient, but there are a large number of instances in which it appears very unlikely that there should have been, and, on the whole, the evidence suggests that the same ideas crop up spontaneously in different people at different times and places. Among the most important of such ideas are the idea of the hero who faces great dangers in order to reach at last to some treasure, the idea of creation and of absolute evil, the image of the wise companion and guide who leads one through dangers and difficulties and the image of a great mother of all men.

The elements of the collective unconscious are most easily seen in dreams and fantasies, because these things are least controlled by a conscious sense of the limits of real life and, as we have said, they are most apparent of all in cases of serious psychoses. They also arise in the consulting-room, where a patient may be consciously and deliberately setting aside his critical, conscious faculty. At the same time there are odd things which occur fairly commonly in everyday life which must also be regarded as manifesting the collective unconscious. For example, a mother or father who has taken his or her parenthood in too strict a fashion, and ruled the family with a rod of iron may react to some act of insurbordination as though it were blasphemy against God; a man may treat some human preceptor as though he were infallible and able to solve every problem which might be encountered; a Church or a party or an –ism may be thought to offer ultimate salvation, a place of present safety, and instructions which can only be disobeyed at one's greatest peril; a woman may appear to her lover to be the most beautiful and wonderful woman who has ever existed. There is always some danger in the manifestations of the collective unconscious, but this does not mean that they never have a proper part to play in a man's life. The examples which have been given are intended to be nothing more than illustrations, no judgement is meant on the value of such manifestations.

The ideas behind those things which are called manifestations of the collective unconscious always have general rather than personal significance.   That is, they are connected with things which happen to everyone—things like having a mother, being born, the warmth, light and fructifying power of the sun, and death.   When this fact is taken in conjunction with the universal occurrence of the same images and ideas it can be seen why Jung uses the term "collective", although it is not at all certain that this is the best term.   He also speaks of the collective unconscious as the "objective unconscious" and the "objective psyche", and he is always at great pains to insist that the collective unconscious is not created during the personal life of particular human beings— in other words the collective unconscious is not formed as a result of the conscious character of an individual, and the individual man cannot hold himself responsible for the character of the collective unconscious which manifests itself in his life.

The Nature of the Human Mind

One can usefully think of the collective unconscious as having the same relationship to the conscious mind as the underlying structure of the human body has to the individual peculiarities of a particular body.   The basic structure and character of the human body is the same in all men, and the organic processes take place in it according to the same pattern, and yet all bodies are not the same body, and some parts of the body vary very much more from one person to another than others. In a rather similar way we can say that the underlying nature of the psyche is the same in all men and women, but that each individual psyche is different from every other psyche. Consciousness and the personal unconscious vary very greatly from person to person, whereas the collective unconscious is very little affected by individual variations. This does not mean that the working of the collective unconscious is exactly the same in every individual, without the least variation, but only that there is very much more that is common in its effect upon different individuals than there is in that of other elements in the psyche: deep down the same basic ideas and tendencies are found in each one of us, however we may differ in the more conscious part of our minds.

Jung frequently refers to the deeper part of the psyche as "objective", and he means a number of things by this. First, he means that it is "objective" in that it does not depend upon the subjective life of the individual. It is what it is because each individual is a human being, not because he is this or that individual. Secondly, he means that the collective unconscious is not controlled by the conscious mind of the individual—it influences our lives according to its own methods, without conscious direction on our part, very much as the internal organs of the body like liver and kidneys carry on with their work without any direction from consciousness, and without the knowledge of consciousness: it is largely for this reason that we have to realise that we cannot hold ourselves responsible for the ideas and images which arise as a result of the activity of the collective unconscious. The third reason why the collective unconscious can be spoken of as "objective" is that it is the same for everybody, and from this point of view it can be compared with the external world in which our lives are led. As conscious individuals we have to order our lives within the framework of the world in which we live, and that world is in an important way the same for everybody—two different people in the same place have to take account of the same buildings and natural features: in a very similar way the collective unconscious provides a psychic background or environment against or within which we have to live our conscious lives, and which is largely the same despite individual differences.

The comparison between the collective unconscious and the external physical environment leads to further consideration. It is not only true that the manifestations of the collective unconscious are remarkably consistent even though they occur in the lives of different individuals, they can also occur as group phenomena. Between the two wars of this century this was very marked in Germany. It would obviously be a mistake to suppose that Hitler imposed his own exaggerated and excessive ideas upon an unwilling mass of Germans; the fact of the matter was that Hitler gave concrete expression to deep inward urges which were striving for expression in Germany as a whole. This dovetailing of the ideas of the demagogue and the unconscious ideas of the people is the secret of all demagogy, and it is one of the things which gives the impression that the same unconscious elements can influence each individual of a group. It is almost as though the individuals are rooted in one psychic substructure which expresses itself through them, and Jung has compared the collective unconscious to a mountain range, of which individual conscious minds are peaks. This idea of *one*, universal collective unconscious can be very useful for talking about many kinds of phenomena which involve more than one person, but we know so little about the ways in which either conscious minds or unconscious psyches can and do act upon one another that it is always possible that mass phenomena may eventually be explained in terms of communication at a deep level of the psyche.

Indentification

It must always be remembered that the collective unconscious has always been and ought to be unconscious. It may be that in the course of human development things which were once in the collective unconscious gradually become part of consciousness, but this is a long and complex process, and over a short period of time there is no question of bringing elements of the collective unconscious into consciousness. The personal unconscious contains psychic elements which should be included in consciousness, but the collective unconscious is the unconscious background which gives depth and force to consciousness. The collective unconscious plays its part in our lives, but it is part of its rôle to be an unseen influence in the background, and if the elements of the collective unconscious do become conscious they are too "big" for consciousness to cope with them.

One could illustrate this by a simple example built round the idea of the "Great Mother". This idea gathers to itself a large number of elements from human experience, in particular the experience of human motherhood on the one hand, and our dependence upon the earth for life and sustenance on the other: we all know such expressions as "mother earth" and "mother nature". The myth of Persephone brings out another aspect of this idea, for Persephone was engulfed in a ravine which opened in the surface of the earth, and this is the idea of the dangerous, devouring mother. Such ideas as these can obviously reach alarming proportions, because they involve the idea of absolute dependence, culminating in complete incorporation within the mother, and this goes far beyond the reality of our everyday living. So long as such an idea remains one among many in the collective unconscious it is checked and balanced by others, but if it comes into consciousness as an actual attitude it distorts a man's life in most undesirable ways. A man can really and truly become "engulfed" in something which he treats as the manifestation of the mother-image. That something may be his own mother, and there are grown men who are entirely absorbed in their own personal mother; or the engulfment may take the form of complete submission to one's physical environment, so that one loses all power of decision and direction of life; or it may lead to a retreat from all the paraphernalia of urban civilisation and the attempt to live a life "close to nature"; or it may take the form of absolute dependence upon a human mother-substitute, possibly a wife.

There is a certain difficulty about the meaning of "conscious" and "consciousness" which needs to be pointed out here. There are occasions when one can become conscious of elements of the collective unconscious and gain tremendous benefit from it, but that does not mean that those elements become part of consciousness. It is highly probable that great artistic work, great scientific discoveries and many other similar things result from the fact that elements of the collective unconscious press forward through consciousness, and in analytical experience people may be faced with the tremendous power of the contents of the collective unconscious. Danger arises if the ego becomes confused, and is unable to realise that these elements "belong" to the unconscious, and attempts to take charge of them as though they could become an integral part of the conscious personality: it is then that they prove too big for the ego, and can cause violent disturbance in a man's life. Great development results from the encounter between consciousness and the collective unconscious if the ego can cope with the situation, if it cannot it is overwhelmed, either being destroyed or else identifying itself with the unconscious elements.

If an element of the collective unconscious erupts into consciousness it has attracted to itself a great deal of psychic energy, and it confronts the ego with a

frightening situation. A relatively weak ego-consciousness is likely to be overthrown, to lose all controlling power in a man's life, so that the man ceases
to be an organised person at all. This leads to
psychosis. A somewhat stronger ego may maintain
itself to some extent, and try to cope with the unconscious element by "identification". This has even
more devastating effects than the overthrow of the ego,
because the individual who identifies with an unconscious element becomes the channel by which that
element exerts influence upon others. To "identify"
means to assume that the unconscious idea belongs
to consciousness, and that the ego has taken control
of it. A man thinks that he has controlled the unconscious element, whereas in fact the unconscious
element has taken control of him. When this happens
a man becomes "inhuman" in quite obvious ways.

A very common form of identification is identification with the idea of the office which one holds. This
is a professional danger of clergy and psychotherapists,
among others. Both these professions require that
a man should stand in the relation of intimate guide to
others, and in doing this it is only too easy for the man
to take to himself qualities which belong to the deep,
unconscious image of the perfect, divine guide. If
such an identification does take place in a man's
mind then he ceases to be able to accept the fact that
his advice may, and sometimes should, be disregarded,
and he expects to be treated as a "special person"—
not, he says, because he is special in himself, but
because of his special function. Naturally psychotherapists are well aware of this danger, and take

pains to ensure that they avoid it, and the very nature of the clergyman's work provides many checks which should save him from it, but even so the danger remains. The doting mother often identifies with the image of the great mother in her relations with her son, and seems entirely unaware of the fact that she has completely engulfed his individuality. There are some truly evil men or women who have identified with deep unconscious elements of evil, and many prophets and reformers have identified with divine elements which should not become part of ego-consciousness. Identification results in the failure to be human in certain areas of one's life, and at the same time the inability to treat other people as human— other people too are expected to submit to the absolute authority of the unconscious element.

Inflation

"Inflation" is the name which is given to the effect of identifying with an element of the collective unconscious. One is, as it were, "blown up" into more than life-size by doing so. Most people who have had experience of psychological analysis have had some experience of the power which an unconscious element can have, and are on their guard against inflation of any kind. There is a serious danger that some of them "overcompensate"—that is, that they are so afraid of identifying with an unconscious element that they do not exert the power in the world that they should. One form of inflation which is very likely to occur in the course of analysis is that of thinking that one has discovered the ultimate truth about the unconscious, and about the working of the human psyche, and this is obviously a mistake; yet Jung has remarked that sometimes workers in psychotherapy have failed to publish important insights for fear that their feeling that they have stumbled upon some valuable truth is nothing more than the effects of inflation. In the course of an analysis inflation may also take the form of thinking that one has developed further than others.

One recognises inflation in someone else by a certain rigidity of thought: upon those topics with which the unconscious element is involved the inflated person will listen to no arguments and no reasons, he KNOWS and there is only one side to the question. Combined with this rigidity there is a contempt for lesser people, who are unable to see the force of the opinions which the inflated person expresses. This can lead to a withdrawal from human contacts, and a complete retirement into oneself. Inwardly inflation is marked by the feeling called "Euphoria". This is a strong sense of inward well-being, which accompanies a feeling of one's own importance. If this becomes a settled attitude it leads to serious trouble, but it is by no means clear that it is always a serious and deplorable matter. Everyone experiences a mild inflation when he learns some new knowledge, or makes some discovery: on such occasions one feels terribly happy, and one is sure that from now on everything will run smoothly and efficiently. Such a feeling can be quite delightful, and is usually perfectly harmless—it quickly passes away one comes up against new problems, and one realises that one still has very much more to learn. The fact is that so long as one retains some critical faculty and one can enjoy euphoria without thinking that it is either lasting or necessary, one has not completely identified with unconscious elements, and inflation has only taken place in part.   Full identification destroys all critical faculties.

When a man fails to recognise the transitory nature of inflation, and tries to hold on to it as a permanent possession, then it becomes a most serious matter.   As we have said he may retire completely into himself to nurse the unconscious element which gives him such delight, or he may be thrown into a series of successive states of great happiness followed by deep misery. In its extreme form this gives rise to "manic-depression", a mental disease in which periods of intense excitement are followed by periods of the deepest gloom.   In the periods of excitement the individual is possessed by an unconscious element (or complex) and by its virtue everything seems true and possible, in the periods of depression the power of the unconscious element is lost, and the world seems to be a grim and unhappy place, presenting problems with which the ego cannot possibly cope.   The excitement and the gloom are equally false to reality.

The Persona

There is another division of the psyche which is of importance in Jungian psychology, and that is the "persona".   From one point of view this lies at the opposite extreme from the collective unconscious, and is closely associated with the ego.   Yet one does not consciously create one's persona, and in so far as it is unconsciously formed it may be mentioned in this chapter on the unconscious.   In order to illustrate the idea of identification we made use of the example of the man who identifies with the unconscious idea of the office which he holds, and such identification leads to inflation by unconscious elements.   At the same time it is obvious that if a man has a part to play in the ordered life of society he must to some extent accept the responsibilities which go with that part. If someone goes to an official for information and direction he will not be pleased if he is entirely misled because that official has a twisted sense of humour, and if a person in an official position exercises his sense of humour at the expense of clients he will soon have to find some other work!   Similarly a lazy person must control his laziness if he is going to hold down a job in a factory.   We can all see that in relation to our jobs we not only have to take what we are into account, we also have to submit to the nature of the job.

This necessity of fitting ourselves to our job is not confined to our work.   We also have to live among other people, within certain social groupings, and we have to take those other people into account.   Moreover, we have some concern about what other people think about us.   As a result we are not only the person that we know ourselves to be inside, we are also the person who presents a certain more or less consistent character to others.   This does not mean that we are two different people, one inwardly and one outwardly (although some people are) because the character that we choose to present to others depends upon our own inward nature—we accept conventional ways of behaviour, but at the same time we select: we do not accept *every* convention of our own immediate social group, but make our individual choice. In other words we do not encounter the world with our "naked" ego, but we relate to the world by means of a personality which expresses our ego, and which is in some way suited to the world with which we have to do. Jung calls this means of relating to the external world "the persona".

The word "persona" is a Greek word which originally meant the masks worn by Greek actors, and in one sense one's persona is the mask which one puts on when one faces the world. Yet the persona is not a deception, it is what we really are in relation to the world. It is in some way like the clothes which we wear in our daily life—they both cover our nakedness and reveal our nature.

CHAPTER VI: PSYCHOLOGICAL TYPES

The Importance of Consciousness

IT sometimes seems as though psychotherapists arc more concerned with the unconscious psyche than with consciousness, and as though their work is entirely a matter of finding out more and more about the depths of the psyche. If one thinks this one is making a very great mistake. It does seem to be true that we cannot go very far in self-knowledge without having to come to terms with some such idea as that of the unconscious, but we only come to realise this by starting with an exploration of consciousness. A psychology which makes use of the idea of the unconscious makes use of it as a something *more*: when we speak of the unconscious ideas and intentions of an individual we are speaking of ideas and intentions which must be taken into account, but which are supplementary to those ideas and intentions of which the man is aware himself. No serious psychotherapist would make the mistake of thinking that conscious ideas and intentions are not important, he only wishes people to realise that there are other things which are equally important. Some people have expressed surprise that in his book *Mysterium Conjunctio* Jung stresses the importance of the ego, but this is only a matter of making explicit something which has always been implicit.

Even when one is talking explicitly about the unconscious one is not evading the importance of consciousness, because the unconscious is only known by its effects, and that means by things which occur in consciousness. Moreover, one is interested in the things which manifest the unconscious because they stand in some relation to conscious life. It may be that they are "odd things" of the kind described earlier, which interfere with our conscious plans and purposes, and it is this ability to interfere with consciousness which makes them important, and which makes the idea of the unconscious important. Or unconscious elements may overthrow consciousness, and then talk about the unconscious is important because a fuller knowledge of what has happened may be of value in restoring a conscious centre to the individual. Again, ideas and attitudes rising out of the unconscious may prove to be very valuable additions to consciousness, and talk about the unconscious helps us to understand more clearly what is happening and why such things are valuable.

When one is confronted with another person, whether one happens to be a psychotherapist or not, one very naturally asks "what sort of person is this?" and when one asks this question one's first concern is with that person's dominant attitude and approach to people and things: that is, one is concerned with his "ego-complex", his conscious approach to life. In order to help oneself in forming an answer to this question one has to have some categories in mind, some

way of classifying people: in other words one has to
have some idea of what different "types" of people
there are.   This does not mean that each individual
can be neatly pigeon-holed, it is only that if one has
some general types in mind one begins to get a clearer
picture of an individual: no one can be exactly classi-
fied, and no two people can be put together in one
clearly-labelled compartment.   Jung faced this problem of types very many years ago, and his examination
of types of people was largely the result of his personal
experience.   At the beginning of his attempt he
undoubtedly had the divergence of his views from those
of Freud very much in mind, and he felt that this was
closely connected with a fundamental difference of
"type".

The Meaning of "Type"

Jung has suggested that we should divide people
into types in two ways which complement one another
—somewhat as we might distinguish fruits both by
their colour and by their hardness or softness.   A fruit
is red, yellow, orange and so on, and also hard or soft,
and a fruit of any colour can be either hard or soft:
Jung claims that people may usually use one or another
Function, and that they may also take one of two
different *Attitudes* to the people and things they meet.
The *Functions* are Thinking, Feeling, Sensation and
Intuition, and the *Attitudes* are Introversion and Extraversion, and each of the four functions may be introverted or extraverted.

A function is a way of coping with and evaluating the things one encounters. For example, several people may look at a stretch of country. One is impressed by the view itself; he is aware of the shapes of colour, and the way that the shades of green merge into one another. Another thinks of it in terms of profitable farming. A third recalls the history of England, and the different races which have lived in that part of the country, and the different social systems which have organised their lives. The fourth thinks how much he would like to settle in a countryside such as the one he looks at. Each of the four values the view in a different way, and the same view means something different to each one of them. Again, one man sets out to establish himself in the world and his job by the efficiency and ruthlessness of his thought; another relies upon his ability to "understand" people and to treat them in the way that will incline them towards his cause. One man plans every interview and conversation in detail beforehand, another leaves an interview to form itself as it goes on. One person allows for the irrational in other people, another expects them to accept what he says if he can show that it is reasonable.

The different functions are all at the disposal of every individual, but for one reason or another we develop one and ignore another. Even so this does not mean that we never use a function which we usually ignore and we may find that it comes into play without any intention on our part, either constituting a valuable addition to what we are at, or else causing considerable confusion. It is not that some people have one function and not another, but that each one of us is more inclined to use one rather than another. When one distinguishes people according to their dominant function one is simply referring to the way in which they most usually behave.

The dominant function is concerned with the way that people deal with the things that interest them, and with what aspect of those things they think important. The other distinction, that between introversion and extraversion, is concerned with people's relationship with the things that interest them. Suppose two people are looking at the same picture. The first person admires the picture for the arrangement and balance of the colours, the technical mastery of the artist and so on: for him it is the picture which is admirable for what it is in itself. The more he looks at the picture the more he becomes aware of its character and of the effort which went into making it. The other person also admires the picture, but he admires it because of what it does to him: as he looks at the picture he is aware of new insights, new attitudes to life, new ranges of feeling, and the more he looks at the picture the less he is aware of what the picture is in itself, and the more he is aware of the inward response which it evokes. Both ways of looking at the picture have dangers when they are carried to an extreme: the first man comes to see in the picture many things which are not really there, that is, that are there for him, but not for other people. This happens because he is completely unaware of his own reaction to the picture. The second man is liable to ignore the importance of the picture, and to become fascinated by what is going on inside him, and to suppose that his response is unique.

Every experience is mixed, something about it is due to the thing which we experience, and something about it is due to what we are in ourselves: we say that it has both an "objective" and a "subjective" aspect. The objective aspect is contributed by the "object"—the person or thing with which we have to do—and the "subjective" aspect is the contribution which we ourselves make to the experience. This means that it is equally wrong to suppose that a particular experience is what it is soley because we are what we are, as it is to suppose that everyone has the same experience in the same situation. The extravert is one who stresses the importance of the object in relation to the total experience, the introvert is one who stresses the importance of the person who has the experience. Putting it another way, the extravert thinks that the people and things which he encounters give value and importance to his life, the introvert thinks that the really important things are connected with the way in which he encounters those things.

Thinking

"Thinking" is rather an unfortunate way of describing one of the main mental functions, because there is a sense in which all that goes on in our minds can be called "thought". It is difficult to think of a better name, and there is some justification for its use in that it refers to that kind of thought .which most people think of as "real" or "proper" thought. Thinking is a "rational" function which compares and relates things, and distinguishes them from one another.

When we use this function we tend to divide a combination of things into separate parts. To "think" about something (in this sense of "think") is to consider how it is made up, and how the parts are related to one another. We are thinking (in this sense) when we think about the way in which one thing causes another, or about the likely effects of a certain action: we are thinking when we arrange things in classes according to categories—when we see, for example, that we can divide animals into those which lay eggs and those which bring forth their young alive: we are thinking when we compare one thing with another, seeing that this is bigger than that, or that this is more useful than that. If one listens to a piece of music and notices the way in which it is constructed, the echoes from other well-known works which are included in it and the aim of the composer, one is making use of the function called "thinking".

The tests designed to test the "Intelligence Quotient" of children are almost exclusively concerned with this function, and for several hundred years European society has regarded this function as the most important one there is. There is some justification for this in that it is by using this function that science and technology have advanced to their present high standard, but it is a foolish and unfortunate attitude in that it creates very great difficulties for those who do not find it easy to use this function. Thinking of this sort is only one of the ways in which we use our minds to cope with life, and those who naturally use them in a different way should not feel that there is something inferior about their thought (in the wider sense). The laws of logic are the account of the way in which our thought proceeds when we use this function.

Feeling

"Feeling" is also an unfortunate choice of name, because we usually connect feeling with emotion, and this is not what is meant. Jung speaks of feeling as being a "rational" function, just as thinking is, and by this he seems to mean that it is a function by which we make judgements about things. But whereas thinking judges the way in which things are connected together and compares them with one another, feeling is concerned with their "value".

The contrast between thinking and feeling can be seen very easily in relation to the ideas of value and importance. If we are using the thinking function we can only make judgements about the value of a thing by connecting it with something else of which we already know the value. For example, if one is planning to build a bridge one must start by knowing what the bridge is for, and how much money is available and what materials can be had: one does not think about these things, one does one's thinking in order to decide upon the best way of building the bridge within the given conditions. Again, by means of thinking one may discover some means of prolonging life, but one can only say that this has value if one already believes that it is of value to prolong life. By means of thinking we may discover how best to achieve certain goals, and in relation to such goals we may be able to value the means which we think out, but we can only do this if we already know the value of the goals.   Feeling is the function which judges value directly.

The nature of feeling is best indicated by the words which are used in connection with it: they are such words as "nice", "nasty", "good", "bad", "beautiful", "ugly".   When one "appreciates" a piece of music, and makes a judgement about its excellence, then one is making a feeling judgement about it, and such a judgement is made upon the piece of music as a whole. When we think about the music we see how it fits together; when we use feeling we are aware of what it is like.   In general feeling is concerned with things in their totality, rather than with the relations between their parts.

Sensation

Thinking and feeling are "rational" functions by means of which we make judgements about things. Sensation is called an "irrational" function because it is neither concerned with relations between things, nor with their value.   Sensation is the function by means of which we become aware of things as they appear. Sensation deals with the shape, colour and arrangement of the things which we see, and it is also concerned with facts.   When we use this function we are not concerned with good and bad, right or wrong, cause and effect or any other relationships or comparisons between things, we are simply concerned with what the actual state of things is.

Just as thinking and feeling are two different ways of making judgements, so sensation is one of two ways in which one becomes aware of what the situation is. The other is intuition, and one can illustrate the difference by thinking of two people who see an accident. The person who uses his sensation function sees what happens. He notices how one car comes round the corner, how it suddenly slows, and the rear wheels begin to skid; he sees the car slew against a lamp post, which is bent over, and he sees it slam into the back of another car parked by the pavement. When he thinks about what he has seen later on he begins to work out how the accident took place, but so long as he is using his sensation function he only becomes aware of the actual course of events.

Intuition

The other person who watches the accident presumably sees the same things as the first person, but he is aware of something rather different. He "sees", as it were, what is going on behind the actual course of events, and the potentialities of the situation. He is aware that the car is coming round the corner too fast, that the driver has to slam on his brakes, and he expects the car to skid. He is conscious, all the time, of the problem with which the driver is faced, and also of the likely consequences of what is happening. It is not that he does not see what happens, but that this is of little importance to him, his interest is in the whys and wherefores of what goes on and the future consequences, not with the actual course of events.   He is inclined to dismiss the things which are noted by the function of sensation as "mere facts" or "mere events".

The second person is using the function of intuition. This is not the ability to jump to conclusions, but the ability to see the inner meaning and significance of what is going on.   This does not mean that intuition is always correct, any more than we can always see accurately and correctly what happens when we use the function of sensation.   The thing is that the intuition function is concerned with a different aspect of what is happening.   The artist who puts on his canvas an almost photographic picture of the landscape at which he looks is using his sensation function, the artist who gives to the landscape a characteristic "atmosphere" and who distorts or varies the actual appearance of that landscape in order to do so, is using his intuition function—he is intuiting and trying to represent the inherent significance of the place.

The Four Functions

It can be useful to represent the four functions by the following diagram—

The functions which stand opposite each other are "opposites", in that they deal with the same kind of thing in different ways. Thus thinking and feeling are both concerned with making judgements, but whereas thinking judges the relations between the parts of a thing, and the way in which they are connected together, feeling is the function which values things. One can hardly treat things in both these ways at once, any more than one can take a watch to pieces to see how it works at the same time as one uses it in order to tell the time. This means that if one is to develop one's feeling function one cannot pay much attention to thinking, and that if one is going to develop thinking one must give little attention to feeling. In a similar way sensation and intuition are both concerned with the nature of things, and they can hardly be used at the same time. If one is concerned with the actual appearance of things, then it is confusing in the extreme if one is also bothered by their significance and meaning, and if significance and meaning are important to one it is only distracting to be asked to consider the exact appearance of things.

The value of the circular arrangement which we have used is that it can be said that a person's dominant attitude lies on the circumference of the circle: one may be dominantly a thinking, intuition, feeling or sensation type, or one may be a mixture of thinking and intuition, thinking and sensation, intuition and feeling or sensation and feeling—but one will not be a mixture of thinking and feeling, or sensation and intuition. Everybody has all four functions, but everybody has developed one or two very much more than the others. We can make use of all four, but we each tend to use the one (or two) that we have developed very much more than we use the others, and we also tend to pay more attention to the results of using our dominant function. The person who uses thinking tends to treat the value-judgements of feeling (his own and other people's) as purely subjective reactions which are probably rather silly, and certainly have no general meaning and importance: the person who most often uses his feeling function thinks that logical thought is dry and arid, a kind of playing with words: the person who uses sensation regards the insights of intuition as a kind of hit-and-miss guesswork; and the person who uses intuition cannot see that there is any value in mere factual knowledge. We speak of a thinking-, sensation-, feeling- or intuition-type to mean a person who most commonly uses a particular function, and who has developed that function more than others.

Some understanding of these different functions and of the type of person which results from the development of this or that function is very important in personal relations, and can prevent many common misunderstandings. Most husbands have been driven half crazy by their failure to understand the value of feeling: when their wives make some remark or suggestion which they do not agree with they demand a reason, and they mean a "thinking" sort of reason. Their wives then try to please by giving the first reason that comes into their heads. The husband patiently points out that this is absurd, and the wife tries out another reason—equally absurd. The husband eventually proves beyond doubt that the original remark or suggestion was wrong, and the wife reluctantly agrees—later it turns out that the wife was right all along, and they can then both see why she was right. Had the husband known about the difference between thinking and feeling he would have realised from the start that his wife might well be right, even though she could give no reason for her claim, and that to ask for a reason was a basic mistake.

The intuition type is also likely to get into trouble when he starts investigating inner causes. One starts with some really horrible bit of behaviour on the part of an individual or a class (the younger generation, for example!) and the intuition type insists on trying to see why and how this kind of behaviour has come about. Very soon he finds that he is being accused of excusing the behaviour, and people say, "but surely you don't think they ought to do that sort of thing!" Of course he does not think so, but he cannot help being deeply concerned about the underlying motives, and it is important that some people should take them seriously —although it is equally important that others should concentrate upon the nature of the outward act in itself. In general we should all be on the look out against making the mistake of expecting other people to conform to the type which we happen to value, and to realise that other approaches have values of their own. There is a real danger of persuading people to use a function which they think is likely to be approved instead of that which is appropriate to them.

Introversion

Many people have great difficulty in understanding what it is that Jung means by introversion. Unfortunately this difficulty besets statistical psychologists almost more than anyone else. The reason why this is unfortunate is that statistical psychologists have concluded that the degree of people's introversion or extraversion can be evaluated by statistical methods, and frequently devise tests to measure this. As a result the idea of introversion in the mind of most people is derived from that of statistical psychologists, and this is a very different idea from that which Jung had in mind when he originally introduced the term.

For example, a simple psychological test for measuring degrees of introversion or extraversion includes the following questions: "Do you butt in on political arguments?" "Do you get very lively when you are with a group of friends?" The idea is that if you say "yes" to questions of this sort you are the sort of person who likes taking part in group activities with other people, the sort of person who is happiest in company and who values being among others—and that if you are that sort of person you are extraverted rather than introverted. The extravert, according to this idea is the sort of person who gets on well with people, enjoys having people round him and does not very much like being alone, and the introvert is the kind of person who is awkward and uncomfortable in a group and who prefers solitude. In popular opinion the distinction is liable to be carried further, and the extravert is thought of as the person who is

unselfishly interested in others, whereas the introvert
is supposed to be selfishly wrapped up in himself.
These ideas have only a very slight connection with
the distinction between introvert and extravert as it is
made by Jung.

The introvert, according to Jung, is a person who
values the inward side of experience more than the
outward, but this does not mean that he values himself
more than he values other people.   As we have seen
Jung insists that there is a part of the psyche which is
just as "objective" as the outer world—that is, it is
something which we come into contact with as other
than our own conscious self, and it is this inner "world"
with which the introvert is concerned.   For example,
an idea is part of the inner world, but it is possible to
value and work for an idea without being in the least
bit selfish: men and women have sacrificed themselves
for ideas just as much as they have for other people, or
for outward institutions.   This concern with ideas
is one of the things which shows the mistake made in
the kind of questions just referred to.   If one tends
to butt in on a political argument this may mean that
one does not like to be out of a group activity going on
around one, but it may also mean that political ideas
seem to one so important that one cannot let them be
discussed by others without making one's own contribution.   Again, if one is lively with one's friends
this may mean that one shares interests in common,
and one's liveliness may come from the interest one
has in the subjects which one discusses with them.

The attitude of the introvert is very difficult for
people who are not usually introverted to understand.

Such people make a very simple distinction between the "subject" and the "object", and they describe as "subjective" everything which is in any way "inside" themselves, and only regard as "objective" the things in the external world.   This is the proper attitude for such people, but from the point of view of the introvert they have identified with their own consciousness many things which do not really belong to it. Because the introvert is concerned with the "inner world" within himself he is able to distinguish very clearly between his ego-consciousness and other psychic drives and powers, and when he values these things he does not suppose that he is giving value to himself. This can often be seen very clearly in the case of people who are devoted to some party or -ism.   If such a person is extraverted he does not distinguish between himself and the idea which he serves, and any criticism of or attack upon that idea is taken as a personal attack upon himself: an introverted person, on the other hand, may defend the idea equally strongly, but he will know that he is defending the idea, and that he is not personally involved in the attack which is made.   The introverted person stands apart from his inner drives and ideas, and is therefore more conscious of them as entities distinct both from himself and from each other.   Thus in solving problems of action and behaviour the introvert finds himself balancing inner drives, principles or motives.   The extravert, on the other hand, is more concerned with the opinions of people around, and with the nature of the different possibilities before him.

Any of the four functions which we have discussed

can be either introverted or extraverted, but each
individual tends to use a particular function in the
same way most of the time.   For example, if someone
has developed his thinking function more than others
he will use it in a predominately introverted or predominately extraverted way, and we can say that a
person who uses his dominant function in an introverted way is an "introverted" type, and a person
who uses his dominant function in an extraverted way
is an "extraverted" type.   We must remember that
whichever type a person is he is also able to take the
other attitude on some occasions, and that when he
uses functions other than his dominant ones he will
almost certainly use them in the opposite way to that
in which he normally uses the dominant ones.   Thus
an extraverted thinking type is liable to use feeling
in an introverted way.   The differences in types may
become clearer if a few remarks are made about the
introverted use of each of the four basic functions.

Introverted Thinking

Introverted thinking is most often concerned with
ideas, and it is marked by the fact that when one thinks
in this way one is only very little concerned with the
relation between ideas and external objects.   It is
the internal arrangement and development of an idea
which is important to the introverted thinking type,
and if he takes note of the way in which such an idea
applies to things it is most often to establish the idea
rather than to learn more about the way things work.
A person of this sort is always in danger of pressing a

scientific theory (for example) far further than the facts justify.   The study which is "a natural" for the introverted thinker is pure mathematics, and the story is told of the pure mathematician in the last century who invented an abstruse calculus: as he put the finishing touches to it he said "there, at last, is a pure work of art—that no physicist can make use of!"

Introverted Feeling

Feeling is concerned with values, and if feeling is introverted it is concerned with the values of the inner world.   Those things which are known by feeling are always hard to communicate to others, because our languages are so dominated by the thinking function: feeling judgements about the inner world are doubly hard to communicate because one cannot point directly to the things about which they are made.   The result is that the introverted feeling type is liable to be noticed far more for his negative feeling-judgements about the external world than for his real and deep positive feeling judgements about the things of the inner world.   Such a person can easily form a habit of retiring into an interior world of his own. Nevertheless he has a very important contribution to make, and if he can feel that another person also values the inner things which seem to him to be of prime importance he can enter into close relationship with that person.

Introverted Sensation

Suppose one is in a Church and the sunlight suddenly strikes through a stained-glass window and falls in a pool of red light on the floor. If one's sensation function is extraverted one's attention is drawn to the window through which the light comes, and one notices its colour and design: one may also admire the way the light falls within the Church. If, however, one's sensation is introverted, then the pool of red light is liable to call up an inner image, possibly of a pool of blood, and one responds to the appearance of the pool with the sort of shudder which might be appropriate to spilt blood. To the introverted sensation type the inner image takes precedence over the outer configuration. Similarly in regard to the facts of a situation introverted sensation records the response which one makes, rather than the characteristics of the things seen or heard. Much modern art is a deliberate attempt to express externally the features of the inner world revealed by introverted sensation.

Introverted Intuition

Introverted intuition goes beyond and behind the facts about the inner world which introverted sensation reveals. Thus one need not stop at the idea of the pool of blood, one's thought probes further, so that one thinks of the blood of the martyrs, and the problems of martyrdom   Or if one is concerned with one's inner response to a situation, then if one uses intuition one sees into the deeper springs of one's attitude—one probes into the pressures and drives which arise from the depths of the psyche, and the goals to which they seem to point. It must be remembered that in doing this, if one is acting in a true introverted way, one also distinguishes these pressures and drives from one's own ego: one sees them as truly objective—that is, as things which happen to one, not as things which one is doing.

Extraversion

The extraverted attitude is one which puts stress and importance upon the external object.   To an extraverted person true reality is to be found in the world in which he finds himself.   His physical environment, his family, the social order around him, the demands which people and things make upon him—these are the things which count, the things which give value to life, and the things with which he must come to terms.

We know very many more people from outside than we do from within, because we can only claim to know one person wholly from within.   This is probably the main reason why we naturally think of introversion and extraversion in terms of a person's reaction to the external world.   What we really notice most is another person's reaction to ourselves, and for that other person we are objects in the external world. From this point of view the introverted person is a person who withdraws from external objects, he holds them (especially us!) at a distance and refuses to become too involved with them.   The extraverted person, on the other hand, relates to objects in the world around, and is continually coming into as close a relationship with them as he can.   Both attitudes are dangerous if carried to an extreme point.   At the extreme of introversion a person loses all touch with the world in which he lives, he becomes entirely unrelated to it and becomes lost in a fantasy life of his own. At the extreme of extraversion a person loses his own view-point: he becomes engulfed in other people and things, and takes on the colour of his environment, whatever it may be.

Extraverted Thinking

When the thinking function is used in an extraverted way ideas are thought of as having value in connection with objects, not in themselves. The introverted thinker will be concerned, for example, with the idea of number in itself, but the extraverted thinker uses number in order to count or arrange objects in the external world. In general ideas are always *of use* for the extraverted thinker, they are the instruments by means of which he describes, relates and categorises the things which he finds outside him. The introverted thinker may look for objects which accord with his ideas, but the extraverted thinker looks for ideas which will be in accord with his experience of objects. The extraverted thinker also pays attention to the thoughts and ideas of those people whom he thinks of as people to be taken seriously, whereas the introverted thinker is interested in people's ideas, without much concern for the status or reputation of the person whose ideas they are.

Extraverted Feeling

We value the people and things that we meet by our feeling function used in an extraverted way. When we do this we do not connect the value which we find in the external world with our own inward response to them (although this may, in fact, affect our judgement) but we regard it as a value which the external object possesses in its own right. A person whose feeling function is extraverted enters very easily into relationships with other people, and is liable to accept the "feeling-tone" of his immediate environment at a particular time without conscious thought or effort. It is probable that in religion introverted feeling leads to a stress upon the inner nature of religious feeling, whereas extraverted feeling leads to a stress upon the symbols and ritual of a cult—that is, the symbols regarded as of special importance by other members of the group.

Extraverted Sensation

It is difficult to see how anyone could survive in the world without using sensation in an extraverted way, at least on some occasions, because it is by this means that we take note of things as they are. By this use of this function we not only become aware of the actual physical arrangement of things in the world around us, we also take note of the state of affairs— the facts of life, in the very widest sense of the phrase. It is obviously essential that one should be able to become aware of things as they are, but if a person is dominated by extraverted sensation there is always the danger that he will become completely engulfed in the march of events, and be unable to stand apart from things and relate to them.

Extraverted Intuition

Intuition is also concerned with things as they are, but when this function is extraverted it differs from sensation in that it reveals to one the inner causes of external events, and the implications for the future which are contained in them. Sensation concentrates on the behaviour of other people, for example, whereas intuition is concerned with their motives, and the likely results of their behaviour. Two general things should be borne in mind. The first is that by means of sensation coupled with thinking one can make judgements about people's motives or the causes underlying events, and also about the likely consequences: in this way one comes to opinions about the same things which intuition reveals to one directly. Secondly one cannot rely upon sensation more than intuition, or vice versa—using our sensation function we may well be mistaken in what we detect as the state of affairs, and using our intuition we may be mistaken about what we understand to be the underlying implications. It is not that one function is more accurate than another, but that they are concerned with different aspects of the world.

Unconscious Functions

The functions are all functions of man, in other words everyone possesses them all in some degree. What happens is that in the course of life one or more is developed as the normal function by means of which one regulates one's attitude to the world in which one lives, and one's behaviour in relation to it. Whether one is more or less extraverted depends upon whether the functions which one has developed are extraverted or introverted.   Since one also possesses the other functions these are unconscious, and Jung claims that it is generally the case that if the consciously developed functions are extraverted then the unconscious functions are introverted, and that if the conscious functions are introverted the unconscious functions are extraverted.

This means that a man who normally uses his thinking function in an introverted way has, in the unconscious, a tendency to use feeling in an extraverted way, and what that means is that when his conscious mind is relaxed or off guard, or thrown out by some crisis or difficulty, he will behave like an extraverted feeling type.   The unconscious function, however, is less developed than conscious functions, so that when the unconscious function becomes active it does so in a confused and even childish way.   That is why, for example, an excellent scientist is often remarkably a-logical, and sometimes actually foolish, when he is not dealing with a scientific subject—he often tends to apply to such a subject one of his undeveloped functions.

The introverted thinking type runs the danger of being carried away by extraverted feeling when he is off guard.   This might mean, for example, that whereas his thinking was clear, precise and original he tended to accept external judgements of value from those among whom he lived, without submitting them to any serious consideration at all.   Again, the extraverted intuition type is open to the danger of being obsessed by inner images and ideas which he becomes aware of through his undeveloped introverted sensation. It sometimes happens that a person who suffers a serious reverse in life gives up his developed conscious function and relies upon a function which was previously undeveloped; this is likely to lead to obsessions and fanaticisms, and probably explains some of the least pleasant phenomena which sometimes occur in connection with religious or political conversion.

Personal Type

It is very useful to have some idea what psychological type one is, but it is not always easy to discover the answer to this question.   One reason is that few people rely exclusively upon one function, and also that most people are extraverted at one time and introverted at another.   Some people are extreme types others are not: some rely exclusively on one function, others use two or three.   It is often easiest to ask oneself what is one's least used function, rather than what function one uses most often.   For example, if one has considerable contempt for "mere facts" and thinks that simply to know what is going on without knowing how or why it is going on, is futile and pointless, then one has a very undeveloped sensation function, and it is likely that intuition is one of one's more developed functions.

One's own personal type also influences the way in which one describes the different types, and it may be of some help to the reader to indicate the personal evaluations which are involved in the foregoing

account.   Intuition, whether introverted or extraverted, seems to be an essential and supremely valuable
function; and it seems (to the writer that is—as we
have said our own values are not necessarily right for
others) that it is always important to be able to see
behind the outward appearance of things, whether
they exist in the outer or the inner world.   Introverted thinking also seems to be an important function,
and to order and relate one's inward ideas seems to be
always desirable.   Extraverted thinking, on the other
hand, seems rather dull and silly, and to be bound up
with mere facts.   Sillier still seems sensation, whether
introverted or extraverted, for this seems to do no
more than record what is there, and to have no special
value beyond that—it is necessary, but it cannot take
one very far.   Feeling seems to be a most valuable
function, especially in an introverted form, but it is
difficult to understand exactly how it works, or how
it can be given a leading position in one's personality.
This brief statement is entirely personal, and is included
to enable the reader to correct for bias in the previous
account, although to some extent that correction has
already been made.   It cannot be said too often that
whatever our own type *all* the functions have their
own value, and that it is essential that some people
should use each of them as their developed, dominant
function.   Sensation seems silly to the writer, but to
a sensation type intuition will seem equally valueless—
not so much silly as unjustified guess-work which may
occasionally hit the mark.   None of us can ever
quite give full value to the functions which we ourselves have not developed.

Chapter VII: PSYCHIC DEVELOPMENT

Readiness to Learn

EVERY teacher knows that learning must be built up by gentle stages, so that the pupil is ready to take in what he is taught. One must begin every explanation in terms which are already familiar, and relate new knowledge to the knowledge which is already possessed. Jung gives a very interesting instance of the way in which the things for which a person is not yet ready simply pass that person by. The parents of a young child gave her various items of information about the conception and birth of her baby brother, because these problems were causing her worry and distress: her younger sister was present at the time, and seemed to be able to understand what it was all about, even joining in the conversation. In time, however, it became apparent that the younger sister had not taken in the ideas at all, and that as she grew older it was necessary that she should be given an explanation for herself.

At any given time there are some things which we are ready to understand, and some which we are not yet able to comprehend. It also seems that we have limits beyond which we cannot comprehend at all, for instance, it is doubtful if everyone is able to understand the higher reaches of mathematics, however gradually he may be led to them. Probably few people ever reach the absolute limit of the knowledge which they are capable of grasping, but nevertheless the indications are that such limits exist, and that they differ with different individuals. It is as though each person has a potential capacity for learning which he may or may not make full use of, and what is true of learning is true of psychic development generally: the range and intensity of possible experience, reaches of thought, depth of feeling, intuitive understanding and clear vision of the world which is possible to a man varies from person to person, and limits are set in every direction. No one, of course, knows with any assurance what his limits are, nor what are the limits of someone else, but it does appear to be fairly certain that limits of this kind do exist.

The psychic development of an individual can be thought of from two points of view. On the one hand we can think of the intensive development of a particular aptitude. We all know about this from our knowledge of modern life: one man developes as an expert technologist, another as a specialist in some science, a third as an artist, a fourth as a business manager and so on, and it is a well-known fact that many specialists are very inadequate in regard to subjects outside their speciality. In the terms which we have been using this is the development of one or more dominant functions at the expense of other functions, and represents the attempt to push the development of that function to its limit. One man may spend a lifetime developing one or two functions, whereas another may reach the limit of possible development very quickly, in relation to his dominant function or functions. The other way of thinking of psychic development is to think of the range of functions developed, rather than the extent to which the development of each one is carried out. This does not mean that all four functions must be developed equally, because it is most likely that the limits of possible development vary between the functions in the same individual, what it means is that as well as developing one's ability in a particular direction one can also widen the range of one's comprehension and knowledge.

Jung speaks of the opposition between these two ways of developing, and uses a rather unfortunate term to refer to the development of one function at the expense of others: he calls this "striving after perfection", whereas he calls the attempt to bring all the functions into play "striving after completion". He uses these terms with special reference to the moral and religious sphere, and speaks of morality and religion as aiming at "perfection" (i.e. the full development of selected virtues) at the expense of "completion" (the full use of the totality of one's being). The reason why these terms are a little unfortunate is that in its proper meaning "perfect" means "fully formed or made" and it could well be applied to what Jung calls "completion".

The Unconscious as Source

Human consciousness today is balanced and complemented by the unconscious. This is how it appears to us from the standpoint of our conscious existence, but in the development of the race (and of the child) psychic life existed before consciousness was developed: in other words, consciousness has developed out of a previous unconscious state.   One can picture the unconscious as originally containing all possibilities of future development, and containing them in such a way that they "balance out".   The relation between psychic elements in the unconscious is such that the activation of one inevitably gives rise to the activation of its opposite, and in a balanced, unconscious state no one element can be developed very far, because it is counteracted by opposing elements.   The development of consciousness is to be thought of as the creation of an unbalance, a disturbance of the unconscious equilibrium resulting from the detachment of psychic elements from their opposites.   This detachment makes conscious development possible, but it also means that the opposites ("left in the unconscious") also acquire compensatory psychic energy of their own.   When unconscious elements acquire psychic energy they begin to press upon consciousness, that is they tend to disturb conscious life and, as it were, demand to be recognised.

It is easy enough to see something of the way in which this dynamism works in ordinary life.   Suppose one has to make some relatively trivial decision— whether to go to the cinema or not, for instance.   First one hesitates, then one make's up one's mind, and then, immediately one has done so, one becomes aware of all kinds of reasons for not doing what one has decided to do.   In small matters this is unimportant, and causes little worry, but in large things it may be very serious.   When a man is converted to a religious belief, for example, it is never long before the "opposites" are aroused, and he becomes liable to be beset by all sorts of doubts and difficulties.   If he can endure this, and accept the values inherent in this "other side" without letting his faith be destroyed he will be all the stronger, but he is more likely to fear to acknowledge such disturbing thoughts.   Such fear means the repression of the unconscious elements, and the converted too often shut their minds to the other side in this way, and that is why they are liable to become fanatics—people who shut out all doubts and difficulties because they cannot afford to take note of them.

Synthesis and Disintegration

A man's conscious personality is a synthesis of psychic elements: that is, the elements which make up that personality are related together in such a way that they reinforce one another, and in order for this to be possible some take precedence over others.   When the desire for pleasure clashes with duty, the good of others with one's own interest, honesty with the possibility of gain and so on one does not usually have to decide the problem on each separate occasion. Most people tend to give predominance (i.e. greater value) to the claim of this or that tendency, and to do it consistently: we can rely upon one man to put duty before pleasure, another continually neglects his duty in the search for pleasure; one is selfish, the other thinks first of others; one man will do anything for money, another is always honest; and so it goes on. This does not mean that there is never a clash, because clashes may occur, for instance, when the usually honest man is offered great gain for a small dishonesty, or when the advantage to himself outweighs an altruistic man's usual concern for others.   The tendency to give greater value to particular tendencies and attitudes only means that for most normal purposes these tendencies and attitudes seem more important than others.   Consciousness is an organised hierarchy of psychic elements.

The synthesis of psychic elements which forms consciousness may be relatively "closed" or relatively "open".   It is closed when a man has established his character to his own liking, and does not believe that any further change is desirable, or even possible. Such a man protects his conscious synthesis in every possible way, and is unwilling to allow new ideas or attitudes to disturb it.   He appears to be a well-balanced, thoroughly consistent individual who "knows his own mind", but the pain which he (unconsciously) takes to protect his conscious synthesis suggests that it is ultimately unstable, and liable to be overthrown if new ideas are admitted.   The conscious synthesis is "open" if the individual is ready to receive new ideas and attempt to relate them to his personality, that is, if he is not afraid to extend his conscious personality, and even revalue the elements which make it up.   Such an attitude suggests a stable consciousness which is strong enough to incorporate novelty without being disrupted.   Nevertheless, however "open" the conscious synthesis may be it is always what a man thinks of as "himself", and this means that he has a vested interest in the continuance of the synthesis as it is, so that if the elements rising out of the unconscious do present a serious threat to it there is always a tendency for him to resist them.

This very natural tendency to resist any kind of violent change to one's character and personality is natural and important, for if we did not have such a tendency we would be in danger of changing our personalities from day to day, until we were no longer sure who or what we were. At the same time this tendency carries with it serious disadvantages, because it means that we are not very ready to receive new psychic elements rising up out of the unconscious. As we have seen the most active and powerful elements in the unconscious are those which are "opposite" to the idea in our conscious minds, and this means that they are just those ideas which seem most likely to break up the synthesis which is our ego-consciousness. It seems very much more satisfactory to develop our conscious ideas further than to admit new ideas which seem to contradict them. Unfortunately there is a limit set to the development of the ideas which are already conscious, and if we persist in developing them without admitting any new ideas, we soon reach a stage at which we are "stuck". A person who has reached this stage may have formed a very satisfactory conscious synthesis, and be a happy and useful member of society, but he no longer continues to develop. There are many people who settle down into a routine of living quite young in life, and become established in their own sphere until they die.

All those who have a serious interest in psycho-therapy, and many other people tend to regard continuing development as the best and proper thing, and it seems that for such people it is. At the same time it is very easy to take an unreasonably superior attitude about this, and to suppose that the person who gets fixed in routine habits at an early age is somehow missing something. In one sense there is no doubt that this is true, but it is true of whatever course one's life follows: if one does not become fixed but develops continually throughout the whole of one's life one misses whatever good there is in getting stuck in a routine early on, and who is to say that one is better than the other? Jung remarks that there are some (fortunate?) people who are never confronted by questions about the meaning of life and their own development, and he adds that if the questions are not asked there is no need to answer them!

The conscious synthesis which gives a man his character is liable to be threatened by new ideas, attitudes and images rising out of the unconscious, and the question with which we are concerned is what should be our attitude to them. If one is content to repress them then one preserves one's conscious synthesis but loses the psychic energy which is bound up in the opposing psychic elements—and there is always the danger that even though they are repressed they will acquire sufficient psychic energy to be able to interfere very seriously in our lives. If we are to make use of these new elements—that is, if they are to play a useful part in our lives—we must accept them. This need to accept the elements which oppose consciousness is an important feature of Jung's psychology, and it is also one which it is not easy to understand clearly. Jung certainly does not wish to suggest that we should simply give way to tendencies which seem to us to be bad or evil, on the other hand he does insist that we should neither pretend that such tendencies do not exist, nor treat them as irritating nuisances which we have to control and nothing more. Acceptance of such things means, first of all, that one sees that they are important elements in our total psychic nature, and, secondly, that one is ready to let them play some part in one's life. It is important neither to dismiss them, nor to suppose that they can be fitted, somehow, into consciousness without any change in one's character.

The real problem is not so much what attitude we should take to the things which oppose our conscious synthesis, as what attitude we take to that synthesis itself. If we are utterly and completely content with ourselves as we are, if we do not think that any change in our psychic nature would be an improvement, then we cannot possibly come to terms with those things which threaten our conscious synthesis. If we are to accept these things we must first be ready to change, we must be prepared to allow our personalities to break up, in order that they may be reformed in such a way that the new things may be included in a new and fuller synthesis. Suppose, for example, that a man has devoted himself to some scientific work, and has formed a habit of giving up pleasure and friendships for the sake of devoting all his attention to his work. If such a man begins to feel drawn to a woman the new attitude will appear to him to endanger his established way of life, and even his character. He thinks of himself as a man wholeheartedly devoted to his work, but he realises that if he is going to take the new thing seriously the woman will be a serious rival to his work, making claims both on his time and on his attention. Moreover, in order to develop his relationship with the woman he will need to make use of aspects of his character quite different from those he has developed in order to carry out his scientific work—that is, of feelings and emotions which he has always despised as things which could only interfere with the way of life which he had chosen. All this means that he has to struggle with himself: he must either give up his habitual way of life, and admit that there is more to living than the scientific devotion which has always been his ideal, or else he must reject the other side of his nature and (probably) the woman as well.

The problem which faces such a man is whether he is able to give up the established synthesis of his conscious mind. If he is, then he can accept the new attitudes and ideas which have been evoked by his attitude to the woman who has come into his life. This does not mean that he must destroy his old character and old way of life, for to do this would be to swing over to "the other side". What it means is that alongside his old ways he will also learn new ways even though there seems to be a conflict between the old and the new. If he does this, then the new attitudes and ideas will be gradually developed until they are as important to him as the old, and it is at this point that the old synthesis disintegrates in order that a new synthesis may be formed. If this can happen (that is, if the man does not now live two separate lives, sometimes using one aspect of his character and sometimes another) he will achieve a fuller conscious development which includes not only all that made up his previous character, but also the new elements of which he had no true awareness before.

Those who go on developing through their lives are continually faced with the formation and disintegration of conscious syntheses. There need be no end to this process, because there is always more in the unconscious which can work up towards consciousness. The formation of such syntheses is not a conscious and deliberate activity, it is something which happens in the course of time as the ideas in consciousness develop. At the same time we have a certain amount of conscious control, in that we can refuse to take note of new ideas coming out of the unconscious. There are many people who are opposed to all talk about psychotherapy and the unconscious just because of this. It sounds as though they are arbitrarily dismissing something that they cannot be bothered to think about, but in reality they are defending their own conscious standpoints against new ideas from the unconscious. They may not be aware of this very clearly, but they do have a sense that the unconscious is dangerous and even evil. It may well be that they are right, and that they are not ready to accept new things from the unconscious without destroying themselves completely.

The acceptance of the new things coming from the unconscious is no easy matter. To begin with they are usually things which seem to us to be trivial, foolish or evil and even to think of accepting them offends our moral sense: secondly, they do not fit with our present picture of ourselves, and we do not like to risk destroying it: thirdly, acceptance must not be uncritical; if we bring ourselves to overcome our antagonism to these things we are in danger of giving up our original conscious attitude in order to give ourselves to the new things because these new things tend to fascinate us: this would not be "development" but simply change. There is also another danger, which is that such acceptance may go no further than adding to our conscious character without creating a new synthesis; that is we may simply form more habits and take up further attitudes without bringing them into close relationships with those which existed before. True acceptance means giving full weight to the new things without giving up the old, and at the same time allowing the psyche to readjust itself in its own time and in its own way. It is by no means certain that everyone is capable of doing this, and it may well be that it is best that many people should never attempt it.

The Choice

The kind of development of which we have been speaking is forced upon some people whether they like it or not—as in the illustration of the devoted scientist whose life was disturbed by a woman. Sometimes it is the interference of activated unconscious elements which forces people to do something—although they would prefer to keep to their established ways they are beset by problems which arise because unconscious elements affect their thought and behaviour.   This is why it is said that a neurosis may often have a purpose: it may drive a person to do something about himself, and so enter on a further development of his psyche which he would not have permitted if he had not been forced to do something about the neurosis.

If one is driven to the further development of one's psyche one can accept or resist, and acceptance or resistance is mainly a question of one's contentment with one's conscious character—that is, with what one thinks of as "I".   Development can only take place if one is prepared to allow the "I" that one knows and loves to be destroyed, in order that a fuller and more developed "I" may take its place.

CHAPTER VIII: ARCHETYPES

The Dynamism of the Unconscious

PSYCHOTHERAPISTS have been led to study the unconscious because of the occurrence of what I have called "odd things". In most people's lives there are occasions when it seems that some perverse imp or devil has got into them, and is bent upon making nonsense of all that they are trying to do: there are also occasions when one seems to be guided by some good spirit, a kind of fairy godmother, which sees that one says or does exactly the right thing, when left to oneself one would have made a terrible mistake. The unconscious is an idea which is used in psychotherapy in order to enable us to deal with things which actually happen in our lives, and because of this the unconscious must be thought of as a source of power. It is not just a box of unwanted psychic elements, it is a continual supply of psychic energy or power.

The personal unconscious, in particular, includes a large number of things which consciousness has rejected. It is obvious that the energy which such things have is not compatible with that of consciousness, because, if it were, they would not have been repressed. They achieve power and energy by joining themselves to other psychic elements in the unconscious, and forming complexes. The complexes of psychic elements in the unconscious are thought of as being formed round a kind of nucleus which acts as a binding force to hold the complex together, and also provides the complex with the energy which it needs in order to influence psychic life.   Jung calls these nuclei "archetypes", and the archetypes are the main psychic elements in the collective unconscious.

Archetypes are the fundamental source of the energy of the human psyche, and they are closely connected with the idea of instincts.   Instincts are mainly concerned with the bodily behaviour of human beings, and when one thinks of the instincts one is thinking of the way in which the human body tends to behave. In thinking of the archetypes one is thinking of the way in which the human mind tends to behave.   It has been suggested that the archetypes are the psychic aspect of the instincts, and this may well be true, but so far no exact relationship between the two has been shown.   Like instincts archetypes are basic to human nature, and are found in everyone.

Archetypal Images

Since they are in the unconscious archetypes are unknown to us.   We can only talk about the way in which archetypes manifest themselves.   It may be that they are best thought of as a way of talking about the tendency of psychic energy to occur in particular forms, because archetypes do not manifest themselves in a "pure" form.   It is not an archetype, but the complex which is grouped round an archetype which manifests itself in imaginative images or by interfering with conscious life.

One can form some idea of the way in which archetypal images express archetypes without expressing them in a pure form by supposing that a number of authors were all provided with the same basic plot, and asked to write a story incorporating it: or that they were each given the outline of a character, and asked to write a story about that character. Each story would vary from the others in the details and in the way in which the plot or character was handled, and yet each story would have the same basic theme. It is the same with archetypes. In ancient and modern religions, in myths throughout the ages, in the dreams of modern people and in fiction of all kinds the same themes occur again and again, but they are always presented in different dress, with individual peculiarities of time and place.

Archetypes and Understanding

The more one is in touch with the archetypes the more psychic energy is available for coping with the business of living, and that is one reason why those who develop conscious functions at the expense of the unconscious tend to become people of fixed and sterile habits. But this is not the only function of the archetypes. Deep within the human psyche is the deposit of the experience of man since his earliest days, and this deposit sums up the experience of the common and recurring elements in human life. The archetypes represent ways by which man comes to comprehend and come to terms with his external environment. For example, men encounter women as part of the

environment in which their lives are lived, and to a
man a woman is both like and unlike himself.   In
order to enter into relationship with women he needs
to have some sort of inner aptitude for understanding
and coming to terms with them, and it is the function
of one of the archetypes to provide him with this.

This function of archetypes reminds one of the simple
secret codes which one learnt in childhood.   One of
these involves a piece of paper with little windows cut
in it: this paper is laid on top of the paper on which
the message is to be written, and the message is written
in the windows; the cut paper is then taken away, and
other words are written between the words of the
message.   In order to decode the message one must
have another piece of paper cut like the first, and
when one places this over the code message only the
true message shows through.   In the same way the
archetypes provide us with images which we project
upon the external world, and by comparing what we
see outwardly with the inward image we come to a
clearer awareness of the outer world.   The archetypes
are not only the source of our psychic power, they are
also the source of our comprehension of the world
in which we live.

Encounters with Archetypes

Unconscious complexes express themselves to consciousness in dreams and fantasies, and they are also
liable to be projected on things in the external world.
This means that it is always possible that one may
"meet" an archetype outside oneself.   This happens,

for example, when archetypes are projected upon a girl so that she appears to possess a beauty and brightness beyond her actual qualities, when a man appears to be wholly evil without any redeeming features or when a man is accepted as a leader whose judgement is infallible and who must be obeyed without doubt or question.   In such instances it is not merely a matter of exaggeration, force and power seem to stream out from the person on whom the archetype is projected, and the person who projects it is unable to use his critical faculty, because the archetype exerts such tremendous fascination upon him.   Projection of archetypes also gives rise to the sense of holiness attaching to places and things, and by projecting the deepest archetypes in this way human beings stand apart from them and relate to them.   Projection of this kind is not something which one chooses to do, like all projection it is something which happens to one, and it has happened throughout human history until the present age.   For a number of reasons it seems to happen less in the modern age than it has in the past, and there is reason to think that this is connected with a change taking place in the human psyche.

Our critical faculty is called into play more easily than that of men and women in the past, largely because the scientific spirit of the times has taken the mystery out of the external world. Natural phenomena which people of earlier ages regarded as the direct activity of God or the gods (for example, the thunder) are now understood scientifically, and our scientific understanding of them prohibits the projection of

archetypes. The archetypes, however, do not cease
to exist because they are no longer projected to the
extent which they were in the past, and it is still
possible to encounter them, but if they are not encountered in the external world in projected form
they must be encountered inwardly. The inward
encounter with archetypes results from their manifestation in archetypal images in consciousness, and
it is marked by the sense of power and fascination
which always goes with the experience of an archetype. One is "bowled over" by the tremendous
force with which one is confronted, one is drawn
towards it, and one is aware of its quality of "other-
ness"—it seems to come out of some other world.

The great difficulty about describing the nature of
an encounter with an archetype is that its significance
for the individual depends upon that individual's pre-
conceived ideas. The truly religious person will
say that it was an encounter with God, or with some
aspect of God: the convinced rationalist will either
be overwhelmed, or else succeed in dismissing the
experience, probably ascribing it to physical ill-
health: "spiritualists" will ascribe it to guiding spirits
and so on. It is only those who use the terms of
Jungian psychology who regard such an experience
as an encounter with an archetype, and it is unfortunate that such people sometimes claim that in doing
this they are recognising the experience for "what it
really is". The fact is that such experiences are
beyond our comprehension, they do take place, and
they can have far-reaching influence on the lives of
those who take them seriously, but one does not have

to talk about archetypes in order to do this. What talk about archetypes does is to enable us to relate such experiences to other things which go on in our lives within the framework provided by Jungian psychology—and this is only one of many possible frameworks within which we can attempt to comprehend human living.

The Shadow and the Devil

The archetype which is most easily understood is that of the "Shadow". This is the dark, other self which exists in each one of us: it is the dreadful and evil person that we might have been if we had not been so careful to put aside all the tendencies within us of which we do not approve. To a large extent it coincides with the personal unconscious. Since conscious judgement is not always correct we can only say that a man's shadow is made up of what he *thinks* is evil, and in actual fact much that is rejected because a man believes it to be evil is really quite as good as anything in consciousness: thus it is not true to say that a man's shadow is evil, we can only say that it is made up of things which he thinks are bad. The shadow appears in dreams as a dark man or woman, and in films and television as the bad man who is finally defeated by the hero.

Jung coined the name "shadow" because this dark side of our character always accompanies us, and always seems to us a dark and unwanted part of our psychic nature. He has also pointed out that only three-dimensional things throw a shadow, and suggested that if we did not have shadows we should be less than fully human. The archetype of the shadow is formed from the things that we have rejected, and if it remains entirely repressed it exerts a most disturbing influence on our lives: we need to be fully aware of all the "bad" things which we might have been, in order that we can subject them to conscious criticism, make use of the psychic energy associated with them and be ready to take responsibility for our own foolishness and bad behaviour. Since the only common fact about the different elements which form the shadow is that they are disliked by our conscious minds we must suppose that there is a deeper archetypal nucleus round which they gather. This nucleus might be described as the archetype of the Devil.

The shadow is a personal matter, and each man's shadow is different from that of other men, because each has a different ideal for himself, and each rejects different things. Yet there are also evils which are regarded as evil by the great majority of men, and there are evil things in the world which we can become aware of if we will. Our understanding of the world in which we live is defective if we are not able to take evil into account, and if we are to take the real trends towards evil (both in the world and in human nature) into account, then we need some such archetype as that of the devil by means of which to comprehend them. The devil is the eternal opponent of whatever seems to men to be right and good, he represents the principle of evil behind the evil act, the sin which is to be hated even though the sinner is loved, absolute evil unmixed with good.   He appears in some form in all religions and in all myths: raised to the status of a god of destruction in Hinduism, relegated to hell in Christianity, and engaged in unending conflict with the god of prosperity in the ancient myths.   It is around this archetype that the things which we repress as evil tend to cluster, and it is from this nucleus that they derive their energy and power.

The Anima and the Animus

The shadow represents the bad self, the man or woman that we might be but do not want to be, and the shadow appears as a male figure in the dreams and imagination of men and as a female figure in the dreams and imagination of women.   It may be said, however, that this is only relatively true.   In so far as the world has long been dominated by the thought of men the archetypal devil which is common to men and women is usually male, and this is likely to influence the more personal figure of evil in women.   As well as the bad self there is in every man a feminine side, and in every woman a masculine side, and for a number of reasons there are many people who are not prepared to accept this other side of themselves.   They do not repress it so much as "bad" but rather as "not proper".   Thus it happens that in the dreams and fantasies of men the shadow is frequently accompanied by the figure of a woman, and Jung has given to this figure (or to the archetype which lies behind it) the name "Anima".

The anima, from a personal point of view, is made up

of a man's feminine side, and also from ideas derived from his experience of actual women. It is usually represented by a desirable, fascinating and somewhat dangerous female to whom the man is strongly attracted, and the archetype is derived from the fact that in all his history man has always been drawn towards women, and is never complete in himself. Thus this archetype of the anima has three aspects.

First, the archetype attracts to itself the feminine side of a man's nature, which he tends to ignore. This includes his inferior functions, and by their association with the archetype they acquire psychic power, so that they are able to press upon consciousness. Since this side of a man is personal to the man it ought to be part of his consciousness, and the feminine aspect of his nature can be detached from the underlying archetype and incorporated in his conscious synthesis. This will not make a man effeminate (unless he gives up his proper masculine character in order to accept the other side) but will add to his character components which will enrich and enliven it. Secondly, the archetype enables a man to apprehend and come to terms with the women whom he meets in the world, and it is from this point of view that trouble may be caused by the repression of feminine aspects of a man's character, and by his past experience. In so far as the archetype has been included in a complex made up of repressed feminity, and by ideas derived from a man's experience of mother, sisters and girl-friends it may tend to distort rather than reveal the nature of actual women with whom he comes into contact. It will have less distorting effect the more successfully a man has detached from the archetype the psychic elements which are personal to him, and which could be fully incorporated in his conscious life.   The third aspect of this archetype is that it holds before us the fact that there is always more.   The woman is another who is needed by the man if he is to fulfil himself, and by a natural association the archetype includes the unfinished or limited aspect of all conscious individual life.   Consciousness needs the unconscious, the individual needs society, man is dependent, relative and always capable of more, and all these things are included in the archetype of the anima.

The anima in man tends to appear as an individual woman, but there does not seem to be a corresponding, single image standing for the related archetype in a woman.   The tendency is for the dreams and imagination of woman to present them with a crowd of male figures, or with a number of relatively individualised men.   This is partly a matter of "compensating" the conscious attitude: women in general tend to give themselves wholeheartedly to one dominating object, whereas men are more inclined to be interested (possibly less deeply) in a number of things, and in the unconscious the situation is reversed.

Since the anima is usually connected with those functions which a man has not developed there is likely to be an undeveloped or childish attitude about it.   This may be apparent in the images which represent it, but it is most apparent when the complex gathered about it is influencing the individual.   Naturally this is more apparent to the observer than to the person concerned. When anima (or Animus in a woman) takes charge the individual acts and speaks as though his personality were not his own, but that of the archetypal complex, which can be regarded as a partial personality. The anima (in a man) behaves in a wholly silly, emotional and unreasonable way, and some men behave like this when a situation gets beyond control of their reason and common-sense. The animus (in a woman) produces a cold reasoning, usually making dogmatic assertions which do not take into account the actual situation in which the woman finds herself.

We are all liable to allow our response to a difficult situation to be directed by an unconscious complex, and in close personal situations in which a man and a woman are involved it is very common for an awkward argument to degenerate into a slanging match between the man's anima and the woman's animus, and this gets neither of them anywhere. It should not be thought, from this, that there is no value in these archetypes. On the contrary they can provide a means of much-needed understanding between the sexes if they are allowed to play their proper part in life. They also play their part in the formation of personal relationships. A man tends to project the anima-complex upon a woman who attracts him, and it is probably the case that this must be so if a real relationship is to be formed at all. This, however, is liable to make the man see the woman as different from (and usually more wonderful than) she really is, and if the relationship is to develop the projection must be withdrawn, so that a clearer

knowledge of the other person can be acquired.   A
similar process happens the other way round, and a
woman projects her animus on a man.

The Great Mother and the Magician

The archetype of the Mother represents the origin
of the individual; first the actual mother, the origin
of the particular life of the particular individual, and
ultimately the earth itself from which all life seems to
spring.   This archetype has two aspects, one benevolent and the other dangerous.   In its benevolent
aspect it represents the cherishing, nourishing and
protective side of mother and earth, in its dangerous
aspect it has the characteristics of engulfing and
overpowering one—just as one may say that having
been given life by the earth we are eventually incorporated in it again at death.   This engulfing aspect
of the mother archetype is often lived out by actual
mothers who carry "cherishing" to such a point that
their child has no chance whatever of living a life of
his own.   The Great Mother archetype includes
ideas connected with love—which, like the archetype,
has more than one aspect.

The Magician is an archetype which gathers
together the male principles which correspond to the
female principles gathered up in the archetype of the
great mother.   The magic wand of the popular
conception of the magician is a phallic staff,   by
means of which he fertilises his surroundings,   and
brings about the beginnings of new life.   In Chinese
thought these two great archetypes are represented
by "Heaven" and "Earth", the one initiating, active,

fertilising, the other receptive, passive and nourishing. The magician gathers round it ideas connected with absolute truth, and the power of knowledge and even of works.   It is the archetype of the power of thought.

Other Archetypes

Archetypes are related to all the deepest workings of the psyche, and also to the fundamental and recurring situations in which human beings find themselves.   It is impossible to make a list of the archetypes; Archetypal images and types of behaviour are marked by the fact that they repeat themselves again and again, and by the fact that they are connected with the presence or release of great psychic energy.   The archetypes mentioned above are intended to be representative, but they only illustrate those archetypes which can be personified in imaginative figures. There are also archetypes which are represented by a series of events rather than individual figures, and these are just as important.   The best example of such archetypes is the myth of the Dying and Rising God, and this archetype also occurs in the legends of those heroes who rescue a great treasure at the end of a journey through deadly perils.

Gods and Demons

The archetypes themselves "belong" in the collective unconscious.   From the unconscious they can exert their influence upon the psyche and give valuable guidance in the difficulties with which a man is confronted.   Their energy can be channelled into consciousness through the psychic elements which form a complex round them, but if this is not allowed to happen (that is, if one refuses to acknowledge those elements and allow them to play their part) then the power of the archetype is liable to become a danger to oneself and to others.

The most obvious danger has been referred to in an earlier chapter, and that is the danger of being possessed by an archetype. When this happens the individual who is possessed becomes both more and less than human. In so far as the power of the archetype is the power of the unconscious the individual becomes more than human, and is identified with the archetype, but in so far as the archetype is only one aspect of human nature he loses the balancing power of the other archetypes and becomes insensible to a whole range of human experience. Those who are possessed in this way become fanatics who have discovered the only final truth, or the very depths of love, and who seek to force everyone else into the pattern of the one archetype which fills the centre of their own life. Direct acquaintance with the archetypes is fraught with the greatest danger.

Jungian psychology teaches the lesson that we should try to become aware of the presence of the archetypes in the unconscious, partly in order that we may allow them to play their part in our lives, and partly in order that we may guard against the danger of having them thrust upon us. There is a good reason why this lesson is especially necessary at the present time. In the past mankind both came to terms with the archetypes and also disassociated himself from them by projecting them upon the earth and the sky, in the form of gods and demons. In general man came to terms with the gods which he had created for himself by rituals and magic, but he also knew that gods and demons could possess a man. Because possession of this kind was "understood" (at least by priests and medicine men), it was far less dangerous than possession by archetypes is today; this is because the man who was possessed (as he supposed) by god or demon had no temptation to identify the power which possessed him with his own ego. Today possession by archetypes is not "understood" in terms of any generally accepted convention, and those who are possessed are liable to suppose that the powers generated are the powers of their own ego. Now that we have lost the safeguards provided by earlier ideas of gods and demons there is a dangerous vacuum in our thought, and psychotherapy may help to provide a means of coming to terms with the phenomena associated with archetypes.

We should not suppose that it is right to project the archetypes into gods and demons, but it is essential to have some framework of thought within which the actual events to which archetypes give rise can be understood. If one does not they run amok. There are real powers within each one of us which can poison not only our own lives, but also the lives of those with whom we live. We favour some and claim them as our own, we reject others and project them upon other people. The most glaring example of this is the gulf between East and West, across which each sees in the other all the evil things which he will not see in himself.

Chapter IX: THE SELF

The Archetype of Deity

MAN has to come to terms with the powers which he encounters, whether these powers are in the external world or within the psyche. The advance of science and technology has been a gradual process of coming to terms with the powers which exist outside man, and one result of this has been that we have learnt to distinguish between inner and outer powers in a way which men and women of earlier ages did not. The alchemists, for example, attempted to come to terms with inner and outer powers at the same time by projecting (as we say today) their inner psychic energies upon their external experiments, and ancient peoples thought that the gods might act in men as well as in the world of nature. It is still possible for us to project inner powers outside ourselves into the idea of external gods but, as a result of our scientific approach, we do not connect such gods with natural phenomena as men did in the past.

The projection of archetypes into the idea of gods or a God leads to serious errors. When one forms the idea of God according to an inner image or power in the psyche one is giving supreme psychic value to that image or power. For example, if one forms one's idea of God according to the pattern of human consciousness one gives supreme value to consciousness at the expense of the unconscious: if one forms one's idea of God on the model of the archetype of the Magician one gives supreme value to the basic masculine aspect of the psyche. These archetypes are incomplete personalities which stress certain aspects of human nature at the expense of the rest, and if they are projected into the idea of God one finishes up with a limited idea of God, and a tendency to reject a large part of the psyche. This is unsatisfactory both from a religious and a psychological point of view. From a religious point of view it means that one is offering worship, respect or devotion to a god who is less complete and more one-sided than a human being, from a psychological point of view it means that one is trying to live with a limited part of one's total nature.

In general we can no longer safely project the archetypes into the idea of gods, but there is one archetype of which this is not true. This archetype is a sort of "archetype of archetypes". Just as the archetypes are the centres of complexes which lie hidden behind the psychic elements which are grouped around them, so this ultimate archetype is, as it were, the nucleus of the total complex which is the psyche, and it lies hidden within and behind the other archetypes. It could be said that it is the archetype which represents and gives expression to the fact that in each individual man the psychic elements which are common to all men are organised and related together in a particular way, in order to give rise to that particular individuality. The other archetypes, the ego-complex which is consciousness and all the psychic elements active in the life of a man can be thought of as partial expressions of this fundamental archetype which lies behind the others.

Jung calls this ultimate and central archetype by many names. He calls it "the Self", and this can lead to confusion if it is not carefully distinguished from "-self", as in "myself", "himself" and so on, because these expressions usually refer to consciousness (the "I" of conscious life) whereas "the Self" refers to the totality of the psyche, conscious and unconscious. Jung also calls this archetype "the Image of God" and "the archetype of Deity", and he tells us that when it is active it expresses itself in ideas and symbols usually connected with the idea of God. He calls it "the archetype of wholeness" because it becomes visibly effective when an individual is moving towards psychic wholeness and completion, and "the archetype of unity" because it points to the possibility of living a life in which the psyche functions as a united whole. Little harm need be done either from a religious or a psychological point of view if the idea of God is formed after the pattern of this archetype.

From a religious point of view the kind of God whom one would accept if one took this archetype as one's pattern is a God in whom all our human problems are resolved, that is one in whom "all things work together for good"; he is a God who is ultimately responsible for the whole range of natural phenomena, and who is related to the evil and suffering in the world as well as to the good and happiness; he is the

One God, united in himself, in whom all things are joined, and there is no aspect of existence which cannot be related to him. From a psychological point of view belief in such a God may or may not be beneficial. It is entirely beneficial if the belief carries with it a real devotion, and a real striving towards the fullness of God himself, for such a belief, psychologically understood, involves the ascription of supreme value to the archetype of the Self. On the other hand if belief in such a God carries with it the idea that God is beyond all human experience, that relationship with him is impossible, and that he is so entirely different from man that no striving towards him is possible, then psychologically understood it means a rejection of the archetype of the Self for all the practical purposes of living.

We have said that one may "form" one's idea of God according to the pattern of an archetype. It should be realised that this is not something which we do by conscious decision and choice. Our idea of God is something which we simply "have" (or do not have), and we have never sat down to decide just what it shall be. One compares a man's idea of God with an archetype, and then speaks of it being formed according to the model of that archetype if the correspondence is sufficiently close.

The Self as Guide

In Chapter 7 we spoke of accepting the "other side", that is the psychic elements which do not fit in with the pattern of consciousness. We said that all that one could do was to hold both sides in consciousness, without giving greater value to either, even though they might seem to be opposed to each other.   We also said that one could not make a conscious effort to relate the two sides in order to form a new synthesis but that if one continued to endure the tension between the two sides such a synthesis was ultimately formed.   One can observe such a process as this in everyday life, and the instance of the devoted scientist whose life was disturbed by his relationship with a woman was given in chapter 7; but it is most easily observed when it occurs in the course of a psychological analysis.

In analysis the patient is likely to become aware of the "other side", and of the conflict between the psychic elements which make it up and his conscious attitude and approach.   If this occurs neither the analyst nor the patient is in a position to decide upon a way in which the two sides can be brought together in a synthesis, and both need to exercise great patience. It is reported as a fact that in such circumstances, the solution of the patient's problem often "arises", without the conscious planning of the patient or analyst, and that when it does it arises in the form of yet a new psychic element which begins to take charge of the process of development.   This "taking charge" has two aspects.   On the one hand the patient gradually begins to find a new way of living which involves the exercise of both sides of his nature at the same time, and on the other hand dreams and images occur in his mind which seem to him to have extraordinary power and importance: they have the quality of demanding attention, interest and even submission. It is often the case that both patient and analyst become aware of the presence of a force or power which does not derive from the conscious thought of either of them, and which is directing the further course of the analysis. It is this power which is undertsood (in the terms of Analytical Psychology) as a manifestation of the Self.

The images and ideas which arise at such a time not only have the quality of demanding attention, they also show features which are related to both sides of the conflict of which the patient is aware. At first sight it seems that the new thing is created out of the opposites which have come into conflict in the patient's mind, and it may well be that this is a valuable way of thinking about the process. It is even more helpful to think of the two sides which are in conflict as aspects of the uniting image or idea which now makes its appearance. In other words to think of the conflicting elements as partial expressions of the Self which is striving to express itself through them.

The Self takes charge of the process of development when one is ready to admit that one's conscious direction of one's life is not the final answer to the mystery of living, and that one must take into account things which seem to contradict one's conscious intention. In other words the Self takes charge when we give up the claim to have complete control. It hardly needs to be said that there is a close parallel between this psychological idea and the religious idea that God takes charge of our lives when we are willing to submit the direction of them to him alone.

The "Wrath" of the Self

There are two kinds of guidance and both can be ascribed equally to God and to the Self.   When a child stretches out his hand towards the fire there comes a point at which the heat becomes really uncomfortable, and the child is hurt.   This warning of pain is "guidance", it guides the child away from the dangerous act of putting his hand in the fire. Christians (and people of many other religions as well) believe that God guides us in this kind of way, as well as by directing our lives if we will let him. In fact it is suggested that if we do not give up the direction of our lives to God we direct them along wrong paths and so come up against the "wrath" of God which, like the child's pain, is intended to turn us away from the wrong direction in which we are going.   When one considers the psychological idea of the Self one can regard its behaviour in a very similar way.

We have already pointed out many times that unconscious psychic elements interfere with our conscious plans and purposes and that this is the main reason why we find that we have to take notice of them.   In saying this we have so far made no attempt to discuss why this should be so, but it is obvious that the reason is that unconscious psychic elements refer to facts about the totality of our nature which are just as important as the facts which we know about in consciousness.   The particular form which interference by the unconscious takes depends upon what

elements happen to be active in the unconscious, but
the possibility of such interference depends upon the
fact that the individual is a whole—and it is this fact
which is expressed by the idea of the archetype of the
Self. This means that the interference with conscious
intention by unconscious elements may be regarded
as an activity of the Self.

Two illustrations can be given of the way in which
the Self can be said to provide the same kind of "negative guidance" which is ascribed to God when one
speaks of his "wrath". Suppose a business man has
very high sexual moral principles, but becomes involved in an affair with his secretary. He makes a
conscious decision about this, and intends to continue
the affair, and in order to do so he has to repress or
devalue his sexual morality. We all know the sort of
argument by which he does this—he speaks to himself
about the importance of personal relationships, the
overruling nature of love and the relativity of moral
judgements, and he tells himself that he will see to it
that his wife does not suffer as a result of his behaviour.
His conscious intention is to carry on the affair and to
keep it secret from his wife, and in order to carry out
this intention he has to put aside one aspect of his own
character—his moral principle. If he now finds
that he continually gets into emotional tangles and
rows with his mistress quite contrary to his intention,
this could be regarded as the effect of his repressed
morality and as the activity of the Self creating
trouble because the man has not acted in accordance
with his total nature. It would be an even more
glaring example of this if the man was normally very

careful but, by a gross act of unnatural carelessness, allowed his wife to find out what was going on.

The second illustration has been mentioned before. If someone refuses to admit that he has "bad" elements within him and sets out to live a life of extreme virtue, then one of two things is likely to happen. He is likely to find either that he gives way to unexpected tendencies to behave in ways in which he thinks are deplorable and so suffers torments of guilt, or else that he develops a neurosis, which interferes continually with his chosen way of life. Such a neurosis can be regarded as a "compensation" for his attempt to live too narrow a life which does not give opportunities for his total nature to develop, and if the man can be persuaded to see it in this light he may be led to a new approach to life and continuing development.

The unconscious always has a "compensatory" tendency, and it is always liable to bring to nothing our attempts to live a one-sided life—whether those attempts are made in the interests of personal pleasure or of strict virtue. This happens because we are far more than our conscious selves, and one-sidedness is the attempt to ignore this inescapable fact. As we have said this fact is expressed by the archetype of the Self, and we are correct in saying that compensation by the unconscious which destroys our conscious intentions is the activity of the Self and that this activity is a negative guidance which can be compared with the religious idea of the "wrath" of God.

The Self as Creator

The development of consciousness is only possible as the result of the acquisition of new conscious psychic elements (ideas, judgements, attitudes and so on), and it can be understood as the coming into consciousness of things which were previously unconscious. From this point of view the unconscious is a storehouse of psychic elements which become conscious one or two at a time and, from a slightly different point of view, it is the power supply which keeps psychic life going. When we speak of the development of the psyche we assume the existence of a conscious mind, to which the unconscious can make contributions, but consciousness itself is the result of development. A new-born child has no self-consciousness whatsoever, and in the first years of its life the consciousness which it possesses is at best intermittent. The development of an organised central consciousness which one thinks of as "I" is part of the period of early growth, and it is not something which one has from the beginning. Consciousness itself must be thought of as "born" out of the unconscious.

Certain suggestions which Dr. Fordham has made bear upon this. In studying the habit of some young children of drawing circles he came to the conclusion that these circles were connected in the child's mind with "I" but he also thought that they were hardly representations of the "I" of ego-consciousness: rather they represented the totality of the self, with the possibility of the development of the adult "I" within

it.   In other words, such circles could be regarded as
representations of the Self, and as symbols of the pro-
tected area in which the development of consciousness
could take place.

The development of consciousness from a state of
unconsciousness is only possible in so far as the unconscious state is somehow the state of an individual.
In other words, from the beginning there is the possibility of individual development inherent in the psyche
of a baby, and it seems certain that however much
circumstances may direct the actual course of development the possibilities latent in the original unconscious
state also exert a determining influence.   When we
think of the Self as an expression of the individual
totality of a person we must see the Self as the origin or
matrix out of which the conscious individual develops,
and when we think of it as the potential wholeness to
which the life of an individual may point we must also
see it as the directing source which guides the development of consciousness.   In this way the Self stands
to the conscious individual both as creator and pre-
server.

The Self as Goal

The individual mind in which a developed consciousness rests upon a background of undeveloped unconscious elements is created by the Self out of the un-
limited potential of an original unconscious state.   It
is also directed towards a complete development, in
which the total psyche will play its part in the life of
the individual.   This goal is not to be understood as

a final state in which everything has become conscious, but rather as a dynamic association between consciousness and the unconscious in which neither has the last word. For this reason it is not a state in which the ego has complete control of everything, but one in which the ego takes its proper place, exercises full responsibility for the activity of consciousness and, at the same time, acknowledges the existence of other determining factors in the psyche. In the final analysis it must be said that the ego is subordinate to the direction of something else.

This something else to which the ego is subordinate is not the unconscious, because if this were so the individual's life would be just as one-sided as it would be if it were directed exclusively by consciousness. The ultimate control is carried out by the totality of the psyche, of which ego-consciousness and the unconscious are both partial expressions. Thus the goal of development is to allow the Self to express itself fully in one's life in whatever way it chooses, and thus the Self stands at the end as goal as well as at the beginning as origin and creator.

The Self as a Power

"The Self" can be regarded as an intellectual idea by means of which it is possible to link together a large variety of things that happen in human life. At first sight there is no connection between, say, a dream in which one enters a formal garden and finds at its centre the statue of a Greek god, and a disastrous act of foolishness which completely spoils an important venture upon which one happens to be engaged, but by using the idea of the Self one can relate them together.   The dream expresses the need to unite the whole of one's personality (represented by the ordered and formal garden) around a controlling centre (represented by the god), and the act of foolishness is a result of neglecting some aspect of one's personality.   The Self manifests itself as a goal in the dream, and in "negative guidance" in the course of waking life.

In this chapter we have tried to show that many different aspects of life can be connected together by this idea, and that many of the most important features of life can be connected together as expressions of, or attitudes to the Self.   Many dreams which we remember as particularly powerful and significant are expressions of the Self, and when we become aware of the insignificance of our own ego-consciousness in comparison with the other powers and forces within the psyche we are taking up an attitude to the Self. As an intellectual idea the Self can best be understood as a way of referring to the essential fact that each one of us is an individual human being, within which manifold powers and possibilities are at work and which can develop in such a way that these powers and possibilities find expression.

If one talks about the Self in this way to those who have had experience of psychological analysis one might be told "You don't know what you are talking about;   the Self is not just an idea, a concept, it is a real thing, an active power which you can only know by experiencing it".   This claim is partly true and partly false. It is partly false because there is no doubt that the Self is an idea in the mind: the Self is said to express itself in a large number of different ways, and the connection between the ways in which it expresses itself is not given in experience. As the illustration at the beginning of this section shows we should not imagine that there was a connection between two different things, both of which we say manifest the activity of the Self, if we did not already have the idea of the Self by means of which to connect them. It is important to realise this and to see the extent to which the Self is an intellectual idea or concept, but at the same time it is equally important to understand in what way the Self must be regarded as an active power.

The Self must be thought of as a power as well as an idea because many of the happenings which are connected together by the idea of the Self are happenings in which we experience the exercise of a power upon us. As a connecting idea the Self has to be treated as the origin of the power which is described as the "activity of the Self", and hence as itself a source of power. A most important, if not *the* most important, use of the idea of the Self is to enable us to think and talk about experiences which involve a dynamic relation between the ego and other forces acting from within the psyche. The ego finds itself up against, or at least in relationship with, psychic forces which make demands upon it or oppose it as obstructive powers, and this is no mere concept or idea but a fact of human experience. One may try to understand such experience by talking about gods and demons, about the One God who governs the universe and in other ways, and one way in which one can talk about them is provided by the idea of the Self.

The use of the idea of the Self to talk about such experiences is an important mark of the difference between Jungian and Freudian psychology. In general, classical Freudian psychology does not employ the idea of anything as absolute as the Self, and within Freudian psychology the experience of psychic forces is understood in terms of individual forces and powers (such as the sexual drive) which can, in principle, be guided and directed by the ego. The account given by Jungian psychology involves the idea of the unknown Self which is not under the control of the ego in any way, but which is itself the ultimate, controlling power within (or around) the psyche. The absolute demand which is usually connected with moral values, but which also arises in some people in connection with their choice of profession or way of life, is rooted in the Self, and the search for a "final succour", a place of security from which to face the dangers of life is a yearning towards the Self. "The Self" is the name which we give to the ultimate power within the psyche which we ignore at our peril.

We all experience the demands, the guidance and the opposition of the Self at one time or another, but naturally it is only those who have learnt to talk in the language of analytical psychology who refer to such experiences by the use of the term "the Self". Others may speak of God, or they may ignore the experiences entirely. This is why the encounter with the Self as a power occurs most frequently in the analytical situation.   Not only does that situation aim at releasing the powers of the unconscious, it is only in that situation that the use of the term "the Self" is to be expected.   In such a situation there may come a time when both the analyst and the analysand become aware that they have to reckon with a power directing their work which is not the conscious will of either of them: it is as though a third party had entered into the situation, and it becomes more and more clear that the fruitful outcome of the work depends upon the extent to which doctor and patient can permit this third party to take control.   The experience is in some sense reminiscent of that of Nebuchadnezzar when he looked into the burning, fiery furnace in which three men had been thrown and saw them walking alive in the company of a fourth "like a Son of the gods".

Chapter X: ANALYSIS

Theory and Practice

THE previous chapters of this book have been about words. Very little has been said about anything which is not the common experience of every one of us, but a great deal has been said about the way in which analytical psychologists use their own special words to talk about such experience. It is certainly true that by using these words to talk about experience they put a new slant upon it as, for example, the use of the word "unconscious" provides a new approach to the "odd things" (such as dreams) which go on in our lives, but words alone do not create experience. Our main object has been to show how the words of psychotherapists tie up with everyday experience.

In one sense it is an accident that psychological language is tied up with everyday experience, although in another sense it is inevitable. The surgeon has his own words to describe the objects within the human body which he encounters in his surgical work, and these words are generally not applicable to our daily life. Most of the time we do not have anything to do with the parts of the body which are disclosed to the surgeon during an operation and so have no occasion to talk about them. The words of psychology were coined in order to speak about the events which take place in the course of psychotherapeutic work, and it might have been that words appropriate for this had little relevance to the sort of things which go on in daily life. However, the psychotherapist has no knife with which to lay open parts of the mind which ought normally to be hidden within, and he can only lay bare the unconscious through the consciousness of the patient, which is the same consciousness with which the patient goes about his everyday life. This is why the psychotherapist's words have application beyond his special work.

It is not to be supposed that in every analysis long discussions are held about archetypes, projection and the other things of which we have spoken. This sort of talk is used when one is talking about psychotherapy, not when one is actually practising it, and it corresponds to medical theory not to what the doctor says to his patient. Discussion in analysis is concerned with the problems and difficulties of the analysand, not with the theories of the analyst. In order to put what has been said in perspective something must be said about psychotherapy itself, that is about the analytical situation. What is psychological analysis? what happens during an analysis? and what is its purpose?

Analysing

If a person who had had no contact with psychotherapists and psychological analysis were asked "Who analyses what?" he would probably say "Well, I suppose the analyst analyses the mind of the patient", and this is what one would expect.   But analytical psychologists do not talk in this way.   The patient says "I am analysing", and he may say "I am analysing with So-and-so".   The doctor is the analyst but he does not say that he analyses his patient, because he knows that it is the patient who is doing the work. The doctor may make a brilliantly true diagnosis of the patient's troubles, he may analyse the situation perfectly but so long as it is only his idea, that is so long as the patient does not agree with what the doctor thinks or says, nothing of any importance has happened.   The patient does the work with the help of the doctor.   Comparing some forms of psycho-therapy with a full analysis an analyst said, "That is telling the patient what he ought to know, analysis is spending years helping the patient to find out for himself what he ought to know".

A Personal Relationship

Classical Freudian psychology (Psycho-Analysis) still tends to work with the idea derived from medicine that a doctor does something for the patient, and in a Freudian analysis the doctor stands apart (so far as he can) in order to bring a detached attitude to his patient's problems.   Whether it is possible for the analyst to do this is a matter of opinion, and Jung insists that whether or not it can be done it is a mistake. According to Jung the relationship which is formed during analysis is one in which the analyst enters into a personal relationship with the patient, and in which the analyst is ready to throw his whole personality into the work.

This personal relationship which forms the analytical situation is different from the usual relationships between people in two ways. The first difference is that it is deliberately intended to be a relationship of "openness" and "acceptance", and it is this which gives it its curative power. In most personal relationships there is, quite properly, an element of reserve: one takes note of the character and tastes of the other person involved, and one does not (if one can help it) do or say things which cause distress to him (or her); on the other side one expects a certain consideration for one's own views. There are also few people who are ready to expose themselves "naked", as it were, to someone else, and this also sets up a barrier in our relationships. The basic principle of the analyst is that nothing the patient says or does shall break the relationship, and the patient must know (or learn in the course of analysis) that however open and unreserved he may be in his self-exposure he will be accepted by the analyst. This openness and acceptance can be a revelation to many people, and it is a most important mark of the analytical situation: the other way in which the relationship differs from most personal relationships is that it is itself an important topic of discussion between the two people who form it.

To a large extent the patient learns about himself and his relationship to other people by examining his relationship with the analyst, but in so far as a true personal relationship has been formed it is not only the patient who contributes to its character: the relationship depends upon the analyst as much as it does upon the patient. This means that the patient cannot form much of an idea about what he has contributed to it unless he also knows a great deal about what the analyst has contributed, and the analyst must help him by attempting to show him this. As a result the analyst must examine his relationship to the patient in order to enable the patient to examine his relationship to the analyst. For example, the patient may well find that he is treating the analyst very much as though he were his father, and it will be very important for him to discover why he is doing this, and how far he is trying to get from the analyst something that he failed to get from his natural father. In such a situation there will be a strong tendency for the analyst to treat the patient as a son or daughter, and even to expect from the patient something which he missed in his relations with his own children, and it is absolutely essential that the analyst should be aware of this, and either ensure that he does not fall into the rôle of father or, if he cannot or does not think he should do this, to make sure that the patient knows what is going on. This, of course, is a very elementary example which applies in some way to the majority of analytical situations.

The Jungian attitude to the nature of the analytical relationship grew out of the experience of analysts, but it is very easy to give a theoretical justification of it. A doctor who is dealing with a physical disease is concerned with the functioning of the body, and to a large extent the body of an individual functions in

the same way wherever he happens to be. This is
not to deny that the mental state of a patient influences
his physical state but, although this is true, a diseased
liver, for example, is not greatly affected by removing
a man from his home to an hospital: the physician or
surgeon is generally able to treat the body in isolation
from the relationships which the patient has with other
people, and with the doctor. The psychological
analyst, on the other hand, is dealing with the personality of his patient, and the human personality is not
something which can be isolated from personal
relationships—it is largely formed by the personal
relationships in which the individual has been involved,
and it is almost entirely expressed within personal
relationships. It follows that any dealings with a
patient which involve his personality must also involve
the relationships which the individual forms, and it is
only if the analyst can work within a real personal
relationship that he can hope to give the patient any
real help in the work of understanding his psyche.

Projection and the "Transference"

Projection inevitably plays an important rôle in
analysis, and it is often only by projecting unconscious
elements upon the analyst that the patient discovers
their existence. At the same time it is very probable
that every close personal relationship involves a great
deal of projection. The difference is that analysis
provides the opportunity of examining what is going
on, so that the analytical relationship becomes a special
relationship which throws light upon all personal

relationships. Many ordinary relationships would be irreparably damaged if one had to examine them in the same way as patient and analyst examine their relationships within the analytical situation.

The patient projects upon the analyst elements of his own psyche of which he is not aware, and he then relates to the analyst as though that element were a personal characteristic of the analyst. For example, suppose that the patient has always tried to be "broad-minded" and not to take a critical attitude to the behaviour of other people. This may mean that he has repressed a considerable tendency to criticise others, and that in order to be broad-minded he has had to fight the temptation to behave like a prim old maid. In such a case the patient may project his old-maidishness upon the analyst, and this sets up a relationship between patient and analyst characterised by a tendency for the analyst to disapprove of the patient, or, at least, to seem to the patient to disapprove of him. In such a situation one of two things happens. If the analyst accepts the rôle of disapproving critic (which is something one would not expect him to do), then he does actually experience disapproval of the things that the patient (unconsciously) wants him to disapprove of, and the patient gets a great kick out of coming and talking about such things so that they can be condemned. In such a situation nothing gets done, and analysis drags on without doing anyone any good. The function of the analyst is to be aware of what is going on, and to refuse to let his real opinions be distorted by projection, so that he can gradually enable the patient to distinguish between what he actually thinks and what he (the patient) has projected upon him. In this way the patient eventually comes to see that the tendency to be critical and old-maidish is his own, and that without giving up his broad-mindedness he must somehow make room for this other side. Incidentally there are as many people who are just as unwilling to accept and come to terms with attitudes like this, as there are who will not acknowledge their unconscious sexual desires.

It should be clearly understood that there is rarely anything crude about projection and that it is a subtle happening which it requires long training to spot. The patient does not normally project just anything on the analyst, he projects things which are appropriate to the particular analyst with whom he is involved. In other words the projection tends to bring out aspects of the analyst's character, and this is why it is only after long training that an analyst is able to distinguish between his own attitude and the attitude which the patient projects upon him. The importance of doing this may lead the analyst into the opposite error: since he is on his guard against accepting the attitude which the patient projects upon him he may falsify his own attitude as a result. For example, if the patient is attempting to project a disapproving attitude upon the analyst the analyst may be in danger of hiding his own real disapproval in order to compensate for the effects of projection, and this can falsify the relationship just as much as the projection itself. The analyst must accept the patient, whatever the patient may say, but this does not mean that he must agree that the patient is right in everything that he does.

"Transference" is a special and very important case of projection, and it plays an important part in very many analytical situations. A transference occurs when the patient projects upon the analyst characteristics which he has, in the past, attributed to his parents (or parent) and so takes to the analyst the attitude that he took to his parents as a child. The main reasons why this should be a fairly common feature of analysis are obvious: first, there is a real parallel between the parent-child relationship and the analyst-patient relationship, because in both one is seeking help and support from the other; secondly, there are large numbers of people whose mental difficulties originated in their childhood, and whose present mental disturbance is due to a failure to enter into proper relationship with their parents in the past. The transference situation in the analysis enables people to recover the problems of their childhood and then to attempt to deal with them in an adult manner.

The transference is said to be either "positive" or "negative", and this is ultimately a reflection of the fact that our attitude to our parents is inevitably two-sided. On the one hand it is essential that the growing child should depend both physically and psychically upon his parents: he must rely upon them for physical necessities, for love and companionship and for direction and guidance; and this is the aspect of the parent-child relationship which is repeated when a positive transference to the analyst sets in. On the other hand the growing child has also to learn to stand on his own feet, to provide his own necessities, to form his own ideas and opinions and to live his own life. In his attempt to do this his parents stand in his way, and they do this whether they themselves try to keep their child dependent upon them or not: to the growing child they represent security and safety from the dangers of life, and he can only learn to live his own life if he is ready to give up the security which they offer, so that, even if he does not have to fight against his actual parents in order to free himself, he still has to fight against his own desire for their continued protection and guidance. From this point of view the parents represent hated enemies which prevent a man from living his own life, and, at the same time, enemies from whom he cannot bear to disassociate himself; this is the aspect of the parent-child relationship which is reflected in a negative transference.

When a positive transference is formed the patient appears completely dependent upon the analyst, he is unwilling to think for himself and appears to listen carefully and intelligently to all that the analyst says. He tries to please the analyst in every way. This appears to be delightful from the analyst's point of view, but in fact it is not at all a satisfactory state of affairs, and is liable to make nonsense of the whole analysis. The purpose of analysis is not to teach the patient one or two useful ideas and habits, but to enable the patient to live his own life as fully as he can. In order to make real use of a positive transference the analyst has to set the patient on his own feet, and he has to do it without withdrawing himself from the patient in such a way that he creates the same emotional shock as that which results from the loss or withdrawal of a loved parent. If a negative transference is formed the patient does not usually leave the analyst, because it reflects the situation in which the child cannot bring himself to leave the security offered by his parents, but although he insists upon continuing the work he violently rejects all that the analyst is and says. In many ways this situation provides a more hopeful basis for useful work than a positive transference, because the patient is, at least, trying to form ideas of his own in opposition to those of the analyst. It is not to be thought that analysis cannot be carried out without a transference forming, but it is a fact that it is formed in a large number of analytical situations.

Analysis is the creation of a situation in which things happen within a personal relationship and in which the things which happen can be watched and examined. For instance, in normal situations one may feel anger and contempt towards someone else, and the result of this is to poison one's relationship with that person, to cause him to defend himself, and to take up an equally aggressive attitude: this, in turn, confirms one in one's attitude to him, and destroys all hope of a profitable relationship. Within analysis if one feels and expresses anger and contempt towards the analyst he does not defend himself by aggressive attitudes or rebuff one, but forces one to examine one's own attitude, and eventually to seek out the origin of it in oneself. This examination and discussion of one's attitude depends upon two things: it depends upon the readiness of the analyst to accept whatever attitude one takes up, and also upon one's own readiness to think about what one is doing. In everyday life it is rare for both these things to apply. It is certainly possible for a person to accept the antagonism of someone else (it is the meaning of Jesus' instruction about "turning the other cheek") and such acceptance certainly has helpful results; unfortunately it does not often happen that when one person is able to accept the antagonism of another the other is ready to subject his antagonism to careful examination.

It should be obvious that the work of an analyst is beset by difficulties and dangers. However much training he has had and for however long he has himself analysed he remains a human being with his own unconscious character and his own repressions. In accepting a personal relationship with his patient he is exposing both himself and his patient to the forces which exist in the unconscious on either side, and these forces can be powerful and dangerous.

The Aim of the Analyst

It is natural that one should ask "What is an analyst trying to do?" and most people who try to get an answer to this question soon experience great frustration. At the beginning the patient knows well enough what he expects from analysing, and that is to get rid of the symptoms which disturb him, but the analyst has a rather different attitude to the work. From the point of view of the analyst the symptoms of the patient are symptoms of a general *malaise* of the psyche, and the analyst is concerned with the psychic development of the patient, and not with particular problems which seem important to the patient— naturally he has to follow the patient in his account of his symptoms, and in his description of his immediate problems, but he also expects to find that the patient's real problems are hidden even from the patient, and that they will only come into the open in the course of the work.   It may happen that after a period the patient's symptoms disappear, and that he wishes to stop analysing, but this is comparatively rare.   It is more common for the patient to find that he is bound to the analytical work and unready to give it up long after he has ceased to be concerned with his original symptoms.

The analyst does not start with the idea of this or that goal to which he hopes to bring the patient.   His attitude is, rather, that there are psychic forces at work within the patient's psyche, that it is because of these forces that the patient has been brought to analysis, and that the object of analysis is to co-operate with them.   The analyst's contribution to the work is not to direct the patient's development but to help the patient to set aside the conscious restrictions and blocks which prevent the forces within him from guiding him in the right way.   The analyst does not think of himself as someone in possession of all the answers to the patient's problem, but as someone who has been called to help the patient, and who is ready to do so to the best of his ability—wherever it is that the patient is going.   As with all professions there are some who become analysts for wrong reasons, but it is clear that the right reason is that a man has been led to take up the work of an analyst by forces beyond his conscious control. Having been led to this work he is then called upon to help this or that particular patient. What effect his help will have he does not know.

There is no such thing as an analysis which has come to a "successful conclusion", there are only analytical situations which have come to an end—possibly because the particular analyst has given the patient all the help that he can, possibly because something has gone wrong with the relationship. Ideally an analysis continues so long as things are going on, that is as long as the relationship between analyst and patient develops, and the patient discovers more about himself. It may well happen that the relationship gets into a groove and that even so the patient insists upon maintaining it: in such a case the patient may be right, and a long fallow period may be necessary before further development can take place, or it may be that he is wrong and that the analysis (with that analyst) should stop. There is no way of settling such questions beforehand, and analyst and patient must judge as best they can: all that one can really say is that an analysis goes on until it stops. One can also say that most people who have taken analysis seriously over a longish period of time have discovered a new approach to living which enables them to deal more adequately with the problems which are set by their encounters with other people.